SAIL ARMY

A Guide to Current U.S. Army Watercraft

By
Stephen Harding

The longest ships in modern Army service until the arrival of the Australian-built HSV-X1 and even longer TSV-1X, the *GEN Frank E. Besson Jr.*-class logistics support vessels were, ironically, based on the design of the Singapore-built Australian roll-on/roll-off cargo vessel *Frances Bay*.

PICTORIAL HISTORIES PUBLISHING COMPANY
713 South Third West
Missoula, Montana 59801

LIBRARY OF CONGRESS
CONTROL NUMBER 2005902229

ISBN 1-57510-117-3

First Printing March 2005

Layout and Design by Paul Henry Crank
Cover Designs by Paul Henry Crank

Back cover:
The tug Fort Stanwix *(ST-903) pulls away from a pier at Fort Eustis, Va.*
U.S. Army photo by Stephen Harding

We have attempted to credit by name all photographers whose work is represented in this volume. If a photo does not have a credit, it is assumed to be courtesy U.S. Army.

A Note on Style:
While this book was edited using Associated Press style, we have deviated in a one key way — we use the Army's system of rank abbreviations (GEN for general, LTG for lieutenant general, COL for colonel, etc.), since several of the vessels covered herein are named in that way.

For Mari, with love.
And, as always, for Sarah
and Ian.

Contents

Foreword

SEVERAL weeks before the March 2003 outbreak of war between Saddam Hussein's Iraq and the U.S.-led anti-Saddam coalition, I stood on a naval pier in Kuwait gazing at one of the oddest looking, yet undeniably impressive, military vessels I'd ever seen.

Watched over by U.S. Navy port-security personnel patrolling the harbor in heavily armed boats, the futuristic-looking, 290-foot-long vessel stood out among the more conventional craft that surrounded her. She rested in the water atop long, sleek catamaran sponsons, her bright natural-aluminum skin glinting in the sun. Banks of large, gleaming windows pierced the sides of her upper works, and she might easily have been mistaken for the starship *Enterprise* if not for the words "U.S. Army" stenciled in large block letters just aft of her wickedly pointed stem.

The ship was the Army theater-support vessel *Spearhead*, and she was in the Persian Gulf as part of a little-known but vital Army watercraft fleet supporting the pre-war buildup of U.S. forces in the region. And though her sleek and eye-catching lines tended to make her the focus of attention wherever she appeared, *Spearhead* was just one member of a larger flotilla that included the entire range of Army watercraft — from unpowered fuel and dry-cargo barges to tugboats, landing craft both large and small, and logistics-support vessels capable of carrying 40 M-1 Abrams tanks at a time.

While some people will be surprised to learn that Army watercraft played a vital role in Operation Iraqi Freedom, most will be stunned simply to know that the Army has operated its own vessels in each of the nation's conflicts since the War of Independence. That the Army's current fleet numbers nearly 250 hulls will come as an even bigger surprise, given that most otherwise-knowledgeable defense experts assume that operating U.S. military watercraft is the sole preserve of the Navy.

In more than 20 years as a defense journalist for publications both civilian and military, I have had an insider's view of the worldwide operations of the Army's watercraft fleet. I have been fortunate to spend time aboard Army vessels in locales as varied as the remote Marshall Islands, Alaska's Inside Passage, southern England, the Persian Gulf and throughout the coastal waters of the United States. In the course of those fascinating if too-brief voyages I have been privileged to meet and come to know many Army mariners, and have gained a deep respect for their professionalism and dedication.

I have also developed a deep and abiding interest in the vessels themselves — from the simplest barge to the high-tech *Spearhead*. Each type of watercraft in the Army's inventory plays a specific role in the deployment and sustainment of the nation's combat power — a role whose importance was demonstrated yet again in Operation Iraqi Freedom — and each, in its own way, contributes to the Army's success both on the battlefield and in its day-to-day, peacetime operations around the globe.

This volume, then, is intended as an introduction to the vessels of the Army's current watercraft fleet and, in a more general way, to the strategic and tactical concepts that shape both the composition and operations of that fleet. It is, I firmly believe, a fleet whose importance to the nation will continue to grow.

Stephen Harding
March 2005

A Brief Introduction to U.S. Army Watercraft

The Army Has Boats?

Though better known for its armored vehicles and attack helicopters, the Army is indeed a major operator of watercraft of all sizes. Crewed by active-duty and reserve-component soldiers, the service's extensive fleet of landing craft, tugboats, high-speed transports and other vessels — currently numbering some 250 hulls — carries out a range of combat, support and humanitarian-aid missions around the world.

These missions include tasks as varied as moving tanks and other equipment around the Persian Gulf in support of ongoing operations in Iraq; supporting ballistic-missile testing in the vast Pacific Ocean; moving active Army, National Guard and Army Reserve assets in Alaska, Hawaii and on both coasts of the continental United States; supporting disaster-relief and counterdrug efforts in the Caribbean; and aiding in an array of scientific-research efforts at home and abroad.

In short, though the vessels of the modern Army's watercraft fleet are specifically charged with the projection and sustainment of the nation's military might (more about which, below), they perform a much wider range of tasks.

Moving the Force

While the origins of the Army's use of watercraft can be traced to the Revolutionary War[1], and while Army mariners served the nation in every conflict between the birth of the nation and the Vietnam War, the service's modern watercraft operations date to the early 1980s.

At the height of the Cold War the cornerstone of American military planning was the idea that U.S. forces in Europe would absorb the first impact of any Soviet attack, giving the Army time to transport massive numbers of troops from the continental United States to the combat zone. Once in theater the troops would link up with prepositioned stocks of armored vehicles and other equipment, and then move into action. Losses in materiel would be made up through the shipment of replacements to Europe aboard fast Navy cargo ships.

A key aspect of this plan was that the Army would be responsible for getting its vehicles and equipment off the ships. This was to be done either by unloading the materiel at established ports or, if the ports were damaged or otherwise unusable, by unloading at sea directly onto lighterage vessels that would carry the equipment to shore.

The problem was that the Army's then-current fleet — Korean War-vintage tugboats, small landing craft and an eclectic assortment of other vessel types — wasn't up to the task. So the service embarked on both a rethinking of its watercraft policies and on the development and acquisition of various specialized types of watercraft. By the late 1980s this effort had resulted in the introduction of both a new strategy of Army watercraft operations — one aimed not at the now-absent Soviet threat but at regional conflicts — and new vessels specifically designed to support that strategy.

LOTS and Intratheater Lift

The strategy the Army developed assumed that in most conflicts established ports would be nonexistent, degraded or denied, and that all vehicles and equipment would have to be brought ashore through what's known as a logistics-over-the-shore, or LOTS, operation (or, if other U.S. military services are involved, a joint LOTS, or JLOTS). In addition, the strategy also assumed that Army watercraft would be responsible for moving vehicles and equipment within a theater of operations, a mission known as intratheater lift.

During a JLOTS mission Navy and commercial cargo vessels anchor offshore and transfer their loads to waiting Army vessels for the trip to the beach. The offloading can be accomplished in two ways: The vehicles can either be hoisted off the cargo ship with cranes, or can drive down a ramp and onto a roll-on/roll-off discharge facility, or RRDF. Essentially a floating wharf secured alongside the cargo vessel, the RRDF allows the

[1] It is one of the great ironies of American military history that the Army had a fleet before the Navy was established. GEN George Washington ordered the creation of a blockading force of small warships manned by soldiers of the Continental Army. The first of these vessels, the 78-ton schooner *Hannah*, was commissioned on Aug. 24, 1775. Seven additional vessels ultimately joined the Army fleet.

off-loaded vehicles to be driven directly aboard waiting Army landing craft. Non-vehicular cargo can also be offloaded by crane or by cargo-handling vehicles that drive it aboard the waiting watercraft.

Once loaded, the Army landing craft put their cargoes ashore directly on the beach or, if the beach conditions don't allow direct landing, can offload the vehicles and other equipment onto a causeway. Essentially a floating roadway, the causeway is anchored to the beach and projects several hundred meters out to sea.

JLOTS operations employ two types of Army landing craft — the smaller LCM-8 and the larger LCU-2000-series vessels — as well as specialized craft that tend the RRDF and causeway. The intratheater lift mission — which entails the transportation of vehicles and equipment over long distances — is undertaken either by the LCU-2000, the much larger logistics support vessel (LSV) or the theater support vessel (TSV).

Other types of Army craft undertake other missions: Tugboats work offshore, in harbors and in inland waterways; modified LCM-8s are used as command-and-control craft and for diving and salvage support; and barges and workboats of various types carry out a range of humdrum but important tasks.

Categories, Units and Missions

The Army's current watercraft fall into three categories: high-speed vessels, lighterage and floating utility.

• High-speed vessels such as the Army-operated TSV and the high speed vessel (HSV) under joint Army-Navy evaluation are designed to provide rapid movement of intact, ready-to-fight units within a theater of operations. Designed to operate independently, high-speed vessels also provide intratheater lift.

• Lighterage craft are used to transport equipment, cargo and personnel between ships, from ship to shore, or along inland waterways. Lighterage is further divided into conventional-displacement landing craft — such as the LSV, LCM-8 and LCU-2000 — and modular causeway systems.

• Floating utility craft perform operations incidental to water terminal operations, except lighterage. Watercraft in this category include harbor and oceangoing tugboats, pusher tugs, floating cranes, barges, floating machine shops,

U.S. Army/Steve Harding

An LCU-2000-class utility landing craft approaches a floating causeway during a JLOTS exercise off Fort Story, Va. The vessel will lower its ramp to discharge vehicles directly onto the causeway.

The larger Army watercraft — including the logistics support vessel — can carry equipment directly to the theater of combat. This LSV is unloading an M-1 main battle tank at the port of Ash Shuyabah, Kuwait.

RRDFs and workboats.

Watercraft units belong to the Transportation Corps and consist of several types.

• TSV detachments provide operational movement and repositioning of intact combat units and follow-on sustainment of forces. Current plans are to organize seperate detachments consisting of one TSV and one complete crew.

• LSV detachments carry cargo or equipment throughout a theater of operations or on intratheater routes not otherwise serviced by the Navy's Military Sealift Command. LSV detachments also assist in roll-on/roll-off or JLOTS operations, particularly with container-handling equipment and oversize or overweight cargo. Each detachment consists of one LSV and one complete crew.

• Heavy boat companies operate LCU-2000-class vessels to transport containers, vehicles or oversize cargo in offshore-discharge operations. The company also undertakes lighterage service in ports and harbors, in inland and coastal waterways, or between islands. Each company consists of 10 LCU-2000s and crews.

• Floating craft companies are capable of heavy tows within a harbor or limited offshore towing between terminals, as well as heavy lifts beyond the capabilities of a ship's gear. Each company consists of three large tugs, four small tugs, two barge derricks (floating cranes), and two barges for deck or liquid cargo.

• Modular causeway companies give the Army the ability to transfer cargo among ships or between ship and shore. Each company has two roll-on/roll-off discharge facilities, one causeway ferry and one floating causeway.

• Watercraft maintenance companies provide marine-maintenance support in any theater. Each company is equipped with one containerized maintenance facility.

Vessel Designations

All Army watercraft types are identified by a one- or two-letter designation indicating the vessel's primary purpose, and named vessels carry the prefix USAV, for U.S. Army vessel. The designations pertaining to the current fleet are:

• Barge, dry-cargo, nonpropelled (100 through 149 feet) – BC

• Conversion kit, barge deck enclosure – BCDK

• Crane, floating (barge derrick) – BD

• Barge, liquid cargo, nonpropelled – BG

• Barge, dry cargo, nonpropelled – BK

• Ferryboat – FB

• Repair shop, floating, marine craft, non-propelled – FMS

- High-speed vessel – HSV
- Boat, utility – J
- Landing craft, mechanized – LCM
- Landing craft, utility – LCU
- Logistics support vessel – LSV
- Tug, large, seagoing – LT
- Tug, small, harbor – ST
- Side-loadable warping tug – SLWT
- Theater support vessel – TSV

The Army Watercraft Master Plan

In December 2002 the Army released the Army Watercraft Master Plan (AWMP), a blueprint for the service's proposed changes in the composition, operation and basing of its watercraft fleet.

While the AWMP covers the various types of watercraft now in service or projected to enter service in the near future and outlines each vessel's specifications and performance, it also discusses the ways in which operational doctrines can or should be changed in order to make the watercraft fleet more responsive to the needs of 21st-century combat commanders.

A particularly important topic, and one the AWMP deals with at length, is the prepositioning and forward-stationing of selected watercraft to make them more responsive to the needs of commanders in certain key areas. For many years the Army prepositioned such watercraft as LCU-2000s, tugboats and floating cranes aboard leased commercial cargo ships such as *American Cormorant* and *Strong Virginian*, which would sail to designated areas and offload the watercraft as necessary.

The practice of prepositioning watercraft (other than causeways and their attendant craft) aboard larger vessels ended in 2003, however, and the AWMP makes the case for forward-stationing selected vessel types. Though the plan is still evolving, it essentially calls for basing one LSV in Kuwait, one somewhere in Europe (most probably at the Army's watercraft facility in Hythe, England) and three in Hawaii. The plan also envisions that U.S. Pacific Command (based in Hawaii) and U.S. Central Command (operating in the Middle East) will each have one dedicated heavy boat company, one floating craft company and one causeway company.

While the extent to which the U.S. government will support the AWMP's recommendations remains to be seen, it does offer a clear and rational blueprint for the ways in which the Army's watercraft fleet can be restructured and better utilized.

Army Watercraft in Action

While the Army's modern watercraft fleet was in many ways a creation of the Cold War, the demise of the Soviet Union ensured that the fleet's operations have all focused on other threats and in other areas.

Operation Just Cause

Perhaps the first post-Cold War test for Army watercraft occurred in Panama during the 1989 American campaign against Manuel Noriega. Army watercraft units had long been based in the Central American nation, and their familiarity with Panama's coastline and waterways proved especially valuable. Missions included support of special-operations forces, ship-to-shore movement of vehicles and equipment, riverine-warfare support, and casualty and prisoner evacuation. The LCM-8s of the 1097th Transportation Company proved especially valuable in landing U.S. troops at various spots along the Panama Canal and the Chagres River.

Operations Desert Shield/Desert Storm

As the United States moved to form a coalition of nations dedicated to ousting Iraqi forces from Kuwait following Saddam Hussein's August 1990 invasion of the small Persian Gulf nation, Army watercraft were tapped to play a key role in the buildup of forces in the region.

Although U.S. and allied forces had the luxury of using two modern, deep-draft Saudi Arabian ports — as well as ports in such other Gulf nations as Qatar — political considerations and civilian workforce restrictions ensured that Army watercraft were kept busy with port operations, JLOTS activities and intratheater transport.

The *GEN Frank S. Besson Jr.* (LSV-1) and *LTG William B. Bunker* (LSV-4) self-deployed to the Persian Gulf from ports in the United States, and carried vehicles, containers and general cargo between ports in the region. LCU-2000s — transported to the region as deck cargo aboard the commercial float-on/float-off vessel *American Cormorant* — conducted more than 300 missions,

For many years the Army prepositioned Army watercraft aboard leased commercial ships such as *American Cormorant*.

among them the movement of Marine Corps equipment between the Saudi Arabian ports of Jubayl and Ras Al Mishab.

The several 100-foot tugs that were deployed to the area of operations proved especially valuable in husbanding the many commercial and military transport ships that called at Saudi ports, moving some 2,500 barges and making 11 offshore tows. Army floating cranes made more than 1,500 heavy lifts, primarily of tracked vehicles, while LCM-8s were used for such missions as command and control, security, diver-support and inner-harbor transport. Also important were the floating causeways used to move equipment from vessel to beach.

In addition to supporting the buildup for war and the subsequent military operations, Army vessels also took part in humanitarian-relief efforts following the liberation of Kuwait. Army LSVs and LCUs delivered food, medicine and temporary housing units during a JLOTS operation conducted near the port of Ash Shuaybah, which had been rendered unusable by Iraq's destruction of port facilities and the sinking of block ships throughout the anchorage. Army floating cranes played a significant role in clearing the port by lifting out much of the debris, and LCUs and LCMs acted as support vessels for Army and Navy dive teams.

Post Desert Storm

Following the end of the first Gulf war Army watercraft continued to provide essential services to deployed forces. During Operation Restore Hope in Somalia, for example, Army LSVs and LCUs undertook intratheater support missions between Somalia and various countries in East Africa.

When U.S. forces were preparing to move into Haiti in 1994 during Operation Uphold Democracy, three LCUs from the Fort Eustis, Va.-based 329th Trans. Co. — *Churubusco* (LCU-2013), *Contreras* (LCU-2015) and *Corinth* (LCU-2016) — transported cargo-handling equipment, vehicles, aircraft fuel and other cargo from Fort Eustis to Great Inagua island in the Bahamas. The island was to be a forward-operating base for

Army aircraft supporting operations in Haiti, and the voyage marked the first time that LCUs had undertaken a blue-water deployment of equipment into a theater of operations. Other LCUs of the 329th and the 97th Trans. companies moved cargo to Haiti itself.

When U.S. and coalition forces moved into Kosovo in 1999 the *GEN Frank S. Besson Jr.* and *SP4 James A. Loux* (LSV-6) ferried vehicles and equipment from Fort Eustis to the Balkans, and then undertook intratheater-support missions between Italy and Albania.

In something of a departure from their normal missions, during the mid-1990s Army watercraft also began to play an increasing important role in supporting ongoing U.S. counterdrug operations. Working primarily in the Caribbean region, several LCUs and LCM-8s have served as mobile operating bases for teams of U.S. law-enforcement officers, as well as transporting vehicles, equipment and personnel among the region's many islands.

Operation Iraqi Freedom

Though overshadowed by the relentlessly televised combat action that took place in the deserts of southern Iraq and, later, in Baghdad itself, the variety of missions undertaken by Army watercraft in the weeks and months leading up to Operation Iraqi Freedom were no less important to the coalition's ultimate victory.

The Fort Eustis-based 24th Trans. Battalion had maintained at least one LSV on-station at Kuwait's main naval base since 2000, and these vessels were among the first to engage in the pre-war buildup. In early 2002 GEN Tommy Franks, head of U.S. Central Command, ordered the LSVs to start transferring important equipment to Kuwait from U.S. warehouses in Qatar, though the effort was kept very low-key to avoid alerting the Iraqis and offending sensitive political sensibilities in the region.

The buildup of watercraft become much more overt in August 2002, when the chartered Dutch semi-submersible cargo ship *Tern* arrived at Fort Eustis to take aboard five LCUs (*Five Forks, Fort Donelson*, *Hormigueros*, *Mechanicsville* and *Molino Del Ray*) of the Army Reserve's 824th Trans. Co., a large tug (*Champagne-Marne*) and a small tug (*Appomattox*) of the 10th Trans. Bn., and five LCM-8s. The soldiers and modular-causeway equipment of the 331st Trans. Co. also deployed.

The TSV-1X *Spearhead* made its operational debut during the buildup, transporting specific types of high-value equipment and significant numbers of troops into the region from elsewhere in the Middle East, Europe and even the continental United States. During the buildup for and execution of Operation Iraqi Freedom the TSV sailed some 30,000 miles and moved cargo equivalent to 1,000 sorties by Air Force C-130 cargo planes.

Just as vital to the war effort were the more than 12 Army-supported JLOTS operations conducted during the buildup and after the outbreak of hostilities. LCUs and LCM-8s moved thousands of tons of ammunition and other supplies ashore from ships, as well as carrying vehicles and personnel.

Nor have the missions undertaken by Army watercraft since the end of formal hostilities in

JO1 Joseph Krypel, USN

***Joint Venture* and *Spearhead* worked together during the buildup to Operation Iraqi Freedom, and are seen here in a Kuwaiti port — watched over by a Coast Guard port-security vessel — just weeks before the outbreak of war.**

U.S. Navy

The shape of things to come? The successes and occasional shortcomings of high-speed craft in Army service, as well as the changing nature of America's worldwide military commitments, will all play a role in determining the size and composition of the Army's future watercraft fleet.

Iraq been any less important. Whether moving ammunition, water, fuel, people or humanitarian-aid supplies, the vessels of the Army's fleet continue to do yeoman work in the Persian Gulf and elsewhere in the region.

And even as the Army continues to transform its fleet — divesting older types and planning for the widespread adoption of TSVs — the soldiers who go to sea continue to prove themselves among the best the Army has to offer.

HIGH-SPEED VESSELS

HSV-X1

While the Army's LCUs and LSVs have repeatedly proved their value in getting significant loads of vehicles and equipment into the areas where they're needed, the vessels have one glaring deficiency — they're slow. With a top speed of less than 20 knots, neither type of ship is capable of providing the high-speed sealift capability often required during the early stages of a conflict.

It is understandable, then, that the Army has long sought faster, more-capable vessels. Though the service's early experiments with air-cushioned landing craft[1] did speed the transfer of cargo from ship to shore, the Army needed a vessel that could transport vehicles and their crews over significant distances at high speeds. This would allow the quick insertion of an initial force, which could then be reinforced by the men and equipment moved into the combat theater aboard Army vessels and Navy sealift ships.

While the Army explored several existing high-speed sealift (HSS) technologies in its search for a faster intratheater sealift capability, it soon became apparent that wave-piercing catamarans (WPCs)

A commercial vessel converted for U.S. military evaluation, *Joint Venture* is a wave-piercing catamaran of a type that is popular with ferry companies worldwide. Her water-jet propulsion system allows her to reach top speeds in excess of 42 knots even when fully loaded.

[1] The Army acquired some 26 LACV-30 hovercraft between 1976 and 1987. Built by Bell Aerospace Textron, the twin-engined craft was classed as a "lighter, air cushion vehicle." It was used to move cargo and vehicles ashore from large cargo ships anchored in the stream, though it ultimately proved too mechanically temperamental for the task, at least as the far as the Army was concerned. The last LACV-30 was withdrawn from service in the early 1990s.

***Joint Venture's* bridge is fitted with state-of-the-art communications, navigation, ship-handling and systems-monitoring equipment. Operational evaluation of these systems allowed the Army to determine which were best suited for use aboard the more advanced theater support vessel.**

offered the greatest potential for military use. Driven at high speeds by water-jet propulsers, WPCs were already in widespread use as commercial car and passenger ferries. Stable and capacious as well as maneuverable, WPCs seemed an obvious choice for closer examination.

Accordingly, in 1997 engineers from the Army's Military Traffic Management Command Transportation Engineering Agency (MTMCTEA) joined with colleagues from the Navy's Military Sealift Command and other agencies to conduct an HSS evaluation. The vessel chosen was a 280-foot-long WPC built by the Australian firm Incat, a longtime leader in the construction of high-speed passenger-carrying catamarans. At the time of the evaluation the ship was being operated as *The Cat* by the Canadian firm Bay Ferries on a route between Bar Harbor, Maine, and Yarmouth, Nova Scotia.

During the course of the evaluation MTMCTEA engineers fitted *The Cat* with a variety of instruments designed to measure acceleration levels at various cargo-stowage locations throughout the ship. In addition, during a 1998 layover in Bar Harbor the ship was loaded with six Humvee utility vehicles and a 5-ton truck belonging to the Maine Army National Guard.

PH2 Frederick McCahan, USN

A Navy MH-60S approaches *Joint Venture*. By operating a variety of helicopter types aboard HSV-X1, Army and Navy evaluators were able to determine not only the best size and placement of the landing deck aboard a high-speed vessel, but also the aircraft-operation parameters.

While evaluators noted that the vessel would need extensive interior modification for fulltime military use, the overall consensus was that a WPC would make an ideal high-speed sealift vessel. This opinion was bolstered by the Royal Australian Navy's successful use of a leased Incat-built WPC — the HMAS *Jervis Bay* — during operations in East Timor in 1999.

In January 2001 the Army approved an operational requirements document (ORD) for an experimental ship to be known as the theater logistic vessel (TLV). The service then sought funding for a demonstration project to be undertaken in conjunction with the Navy, Marine Corps and Coast Guard. Following an intensely competitive bidding process, in October 2001 the U.S. Army Tank-Automotive and Armaments Command (TACOM) signed a two-year lease agreement for another Incat-built vessel for the demonstration project.

That vessel was Incat's hull number 050, built in November 1998. A futuristic-looking craft consisting of two slender aluminum hulls connected by a center cargo-carrying section, the vessel is powered by four marine diesel engines driving water jets. After being withdrawn from commercial service, hull 050 was returned to Incat's yards in Hobart, Tasmania, where it was fitted with a helicopter-landing deck and other modifications meant to bring it up to military standards.

When the modifications were complete Incat's hull 050 was christened HSV-X1 (high speed vessel, experimental, number 1) *Joint Venture*. For the next four months a Navy crew evaluated the vessel's potential as a countermine, special-operations support and anti-submarine warfare platform during operations from the Mediterranean to Norway.

The Army's turn came in March 2002 when the Navy handed over control of *Joint Venture* during a ceremony in Rota, Spain. Manned by soldiers from the 7th Transportation Group at Fort Eustis, Va., the

Sited directly above the after section of *Joint Venture's* main vehicle-storage area, the flight deck also overlaps the vehicle ramp fitted to the starboard side of the vessel's stern. Note the rigid inflatable boat rigged to its launch boom just below the flight deck.

Prospective Army and Navy crewmembers practice using *Joint Venture's* aircraft-style escape slide during training at Incat's Hobart, Tasmania, facility. The slide allows rapid evacuation of the vessel's upper manned spaces, including both the passenger areas and the bridge.

PH2 Frederick McCahan, USN

ship transited the Suez Canal and continued on into the Persian Gulf. For the next two months *Joint Venture* moved all types of cargo in support of Operation Enduring Freedom — the United States' war against terrorism that began following the Sept. 11, 2001, attacks on the World Trade Center and Pentagon. In its final mission in the region the ship left the Gulf through the Strait of Hormuz, delivered cargo in the United Arab Emirates, then sailed for the U.S. West Coast via Kwajalein Atoll and Hawaii.

The Army-Navy evaluation of *Joint Venture* continued following the ship's return from the Middle

U.S. Army/Steve Harding

Stryker wheeled fighting vehicles of the Fort Lewis, Wash.-based 3rd Brigade, 2nd Infantry Division, are securely chained down inside *Joint Venture* during a voyage from Port Hueneme, Calif., to Tacoma, Wash., in August 2002. The vehicles had taken part in Exercise Millennium Challenge.

East, with operational control of the vessel alternating between the Army and Navy. While under Army control in August 2002 the vessel publicly demonstrated its intratheater lift capability by carrying 14 Stryker wheeled combat vehicles, support equipment and personnel from Port Hueneme, Calif., to Fort Lewis, Wash., at the conclusion of a huge training exercise at Fort Irwin, Calif.

Joint Venture again proved her real-world value during the build-up that proceeded Operation Iraqi Freedom, the March 2003 U.S. invasion of Iraq. In the months leading up to the outbreak of war the vessel transported vehicles, equipment and personnel from the United States to Kuwait, Qatar and other areas in the Persian Gulf, as well as shifting cargo between ports in the region. At one point in January 2003 *Joint Venture* and her larger and more capable colleague, the Army's theater support vessel TSV-1X *Spearhead* (which see), were both operating in the region.

HSV-X1 operated under Navy control for much of Operation Iraqi Freedom, serving both in its more conventional cargo-transport role and as a special-operations support vessel. It excelled in both tasks, and it was with some reluctance that the Navy handed *Joint Venture* back over to the Army on Aug. 18, 2003 in Hobart, Tasmania.

The ship had been operating in the Persian Gulf for more than six months, and after the extension of her lease period and subsequent acceptance by an Army crew made up of soldiers from the 7th Trans. Group and U.S. Army, Pacific, *Joint Venture* went into the Inca yards for an abbreviated maintenance cycle. During sea trails after her yard period the vessel achieved an historic first, becoming the first Army vessel since the Vietnam War to be certified capable of helicopter flight-deck operations.

Over the following months *Joint Venture* continued to sail for both the Army and the Navy participating in a variety of exercises and real-world operations intended to further evaluate the military potential of wave-piercing catamarans. In the course of one exercise, held in Korea in March 2004, HSV-X1 made history when Army UH-60 Black Hawk

Sitting in a floating dry dock during a maintenance period, *Joint Venture* shows off her sharply pointed sponsons. The large open area just forward of the passenger area gives access to the forward part of the main cargo/vehicle hold.

U.S. Navy

Symbolizing the joint nature of HSV-X1's initial evaluation, a soldier and a sailor share guard duties during a port call in California. They're standing on the vessel's extended vehicle ramp, which folds upward when not in use.

helicopters landed aboard her while she was under Army control and underway — the first time in more than 30 years that Army aircraft had landed aboard an Army vessel.

While *Joint Venture* has undoubtedly made vital contributions to the nation's security since her 2001 entrance into military service, her work as test platform has been equally important. The Army and Navy have both used the engineering, performance and operational data gathered about the vessel to fine-tune their requirements for follow-on ships — in the Army's case the theater support vessel *Spearhead*, and in the Navy's case the similar HSV-2 *Swift*. And though *Joint Venture's* future as a military vessel remains uncertain — she will most probably be returned to Incat for reconversion to commercial standard following the end of her current lease period — her contributions to the modernization of the Army's watercraft doctrine and fleet are undeniable.

Specifications

Builders:	Incat Tasmania Pty. Ltd, Hobart, Tasmania, Australia
Length overall:	313 ft.
Beam:	87 ft. 4 in.
Draft:	12 ft.
Dead weight:	815 short tons
Deck space:	22,964 sq. ft.
Passenger capacity:	280
Propulsion (main): Water jets:	4 Caterpillar 3618 diesels 4 Lips 150D
Speed:	42 knots (loaded) 50 knots (light)
Crew:	28-32
Armament:	Various combinations of .50-caliber M-2 and 5.56mm M-249 machine guns, as well as Mk.19 automatic grenade launchers and crewmembers' M-16 rifles.

TSV-1X

If the LSV and LCU are the Army's long-serving and capable maritime workhorses, the theater support vessel TSV-1X *Spearhead* is the service's elegant thoroughbred. Built for speed, the TSV is also quite possibly the forerunner of a number of similar ships that will one day replace the older, more mundane vessels that now form the backbone of the Army fleet.

Like the earlier HSV-X1, *Spearhead* is a wave-piercing catamaran whose water-jet propulsion and futuristic design allow it to reach speeds in excess of 50 knots. And while the TSV was built in the same Incat yards that produced *Joint Venture*, *Spearhead* incorporates far more military-specific features and is wholly under Army control.

The Army's acquisition of TSV-1X originated in January 2000, when the service approved an operational requirements document (ORD) for a prototype theater support vessel similar to, but more capable than, the earlier HSV-X1. In September 2002 the Office of the Secretary of Defense approved the Army's request to lease and operate a TSV as part of an Advanced Concept Technology Demonstration (ACTD), and soon thereafter the Army signed a three-year charter agreement with Incat through its U.S.-based partner, Bollinger/Incat USA.

Built as Incat's hull 060, *Spearhead* underwent six weeks of technical and structural modifications based on lessons learned from the operational use of *Joint Venture*. These included the installation of troop facilities and crew accommodations, some 400 recessed deck tie downs, improved galley equipment and seating for some 300 embarked passengers. The vessel was also fitted with a two-part, hydraulically operated, slewing stern-quarter ramp that allows the on- and offload of vehicles (including M1A1 Abrams tanks), troops and equipment directly from the main cargo deck.

The Army accepted *Spearhead* in Hobart in November 2002 and, crewed by soldiers from the Fort

An impressive vessel from any angle, *Spearhead* shows off her rakish stem while maneuvering in the port of Ash Shuyabah, Kuwait. The same water-jet propulsion system that allows her to reach high speeds at sea makes the vessel extremely maneuverable even in tight anchorages.

U.S. Army/Steve Harding

(Above) **Crew members walk through *Spearhead's* 14,070-square-foot vehicle/cargo hold. Vehicles and trailers are driven aboard using the retractable stern ramp, and are then parked outboard of the central structural supports. The vessel carries its own forklifts for cargo handling.**

(Right) **A crew member mans one of *Spearhead's* .50-caliber machine guns as the vessel maneuvers in a Kuwaiti port during 2003. The ship also carries smaller-caliber M-249 machine guns, 40mm Mk. 19 automatic grenade launchers and a variety of other small arms.**

PH1 Brien Aho, USN

Eustis-based 24th Transportation Battalion's 469th Trans. Company, she soon sailed for the Middle East. While en route to Kuwait, the vessel's first port of call, *Spearhead's* crew continued training on the ship's sophisticated navigation and communications systems. And, in a nod to the reality of operations in a potential war zone, the crew also mounted the vessel's defensive weaponry — a mix of .50-caliber M2 heavy machine guns, Mk. 19 40mm automatic grenade launchers and M-249 machine guns. This arsenal was supplemented by some 10 M-16 rifles, two combat shotguns and several 9mm Beretta pistols.

Over the following months *Spearhead* voyaged throughout the U.S. Central Command's vast theater of operations, carrying troops, vehicles and equipment among ports in Qatar, Kuwait and elsewhere in the Persian Gulf. Following the March 2003 U.S. invasion of Iraq she also ranged farther afield, visiting such

PH1 Brien Aho, USN

A *Spearhead* crewmember lowers the vessel's articulated vehicle ramp toward a Kuwaiti pier just prior to off-loading a cargo of vehicles in 2003. The ramp has been upgraded several times in order to allow it to bear the weight of the largest tactical vehicles.

remote locations as Djibouti and Diego Garcia, the joint U.S.-British island stronghold in the Indian Ocean. Nor did *Spearhead's* real-world operations end with the fall of Saddam Hussein, for she continued to support ongoing coalition operations in Iraq through the delivery of such badly needed items as armored Humvee wheeled utility vehicles, 32 of which she transported from Fort Eustis to Kuwait in May 2004.

While real-world operations in support of U.S. military efforts in Southwest Asia understandably have continued to take up much of *Spearhead's* time, the vessel has also continued to serve as a testbed for what the Army calls the "Objective TSV." That vessel, which has yet to be designed, will incorporate all of the lessons learned aboard both *Joint Venture* and *Spearhead*. While the precise hullform of the Objective TSV has yet to be determined, it's reasonable to assume that the Army's very positive experiences with wave-piercing catamarans will greatly influence the final design choice.

In the December 2002 Army Watercraft Master Plan the service anticipated a need for 24 "final-design"

TSVs, though the actual number could be reduced as operational capability is balanced among the TSVs, LSVs and LCUs. And while the Objective TSV will replace some of the LSVs and LCUs, both types will remain in service for the foreseeable future to provide the close-inshore and to-the-beach capability the Objective TSV will not offer.

The first Objective TSV is currently scheduled to enter service in fiscal year 2006, with a total of 10 in service by fiscal year 2017.

Spearhead's main cargo deck is packed with palletized cargo during a 2003 voyage. The deck in this area has been fitted with aircraft-style floor rollers to facilitate the rapid loading and unloading of pallets and other modular cargo containers.

Specifications

Builders:	Incat Tasmania Pty. Ltd., Hobart, Tasmania, Australia
Length overall:	318 ft. 11 in.
Beam:	87 ft. 4 in.
Draft:	11 ft. 3 in.
Dead weight:	820 short tons
Cargo area:	14,070 sq. ft.
Passengers:	363
Propulsion: Main engines:	4 Ruston 20RK270 marine diesels
Water jets:	4 Lips 120E
Speed:	38 knots (loaded)
	42 knots (light)
Crew:	25-45

***(Left)* The Army Watercraft Master Plan envisions a fleet of 24 final-design TSVs, all of which will benefit from the lessons the Army has learned through the operational use of *Spearhead*. She herself is set to remain in service for several years, serving as both an operational vessel and a training platform.**

LIGHTERAGE CRAFT

LCM-8

The ramp-equipped small landing craft is perhaps the most easily recognized of all Army vessels, given the general public's familiarity with the type through newsreels and documentary footage of World War II American amphibious landings in Europe and the Pacific. In Army service, however, the vessel's purpose is not to land combat troops on a hostile beach under fire, but rather to move vehicles and equipment from ship to shore, ship to ship, or within harbors and along inland waterways.

The Army has used several types of "landing craft, mechanized" since the end of WWII. These have included both the LCM-6 and earlier versions of the larger and more capable LCM-8. The Modification (Mod.) 0 variant of the LCM-8 entered Army service in 1954, and was followed in 1967 by the more capable Mod. 1 version. Both variants saw extensive service in Vietnam in the traditional role and, on occasion, in such other, more exotic missions as floating artillery battery and river gunboat (though virtually all organized riverine missions involving modified landing craft were undertaken by the Navy). The LCM-8 has provided yeoman service to the Army in each of the nation's conflicts since its introduction, most recently in Operation Iraqi Freedom.

While the LCM-8s in Army service are not intended to land combat troops on hostile beaches under fire, they have been widely used to move soldiers along inland waterways (especially in Panama). Each vessel can embark well over 80 troops in its capacious well deck.

PH1 J. Elliott, USN

An LCM-8 puts ashore an earth mover and an amphibious lighter vehicle known as a LARC (a type no longer in Army use). The tires hung along the vessel's sides are improvised fenders, a necessary addition when the landing craft are operating alongside a roll-on/roll-off discharge facility.

The compact LCM-8 can be transported by Army logistics support vessels (LSVs) and LCU-2000-class utility landing craft, comparable Navy vessels, and commercial bulk carriers and heavy-lift ships. Ruggedly built, the LCM-8 is intended for use in rough or exposed waters, and is capable of operating through breakers and grounding on and withdrawing from beaches. The bow ramp permits roll-on/roll-off operations with both wheeled and tracked vehicles.

In current use the LCM-8 is assigned to Army medium-boat companies, and is tasked with a range of roles both as part of LOTS missions and general utility work. The former can include moving tracked and wheeled vehicles ashore from cargo vessels anchored offshore, while the latter encompasses a variety of tasks.

In Alaska, for example, Army Reserve LCM-8s fitted with expanded (and well-heated) crew quarters overcome the absence of extensive road networks by moving National Guard and Reserve troops and equipment via inland waterway, especially in the southeast part of the state.

And in the Pacific, LCM-8s fitted with sun awnings transport hundreds of Marshallese workers each day among the islands of Kwajalein Atoll in support of U.S. missile testing centered around the Ronald Reagan Ballistic Missile Defense Test Site. Two other LCM-8s from the Kwajalein marine fleet are based at Wake Island to act as cargo-handling lighters for Military Sealift Command vessels that resupply the island every six months. The bow ramp on one of the Kwajalein boats (LCM-8614) has been replaced by additional fendering so the vessel can assist in the berthing of larger vessels, in addition to its passenger-transportation role.

In a case of what might be called teaching an old dog a new trick, the Army has modified six standard LCM-8 Mod. 1 vessels to Mod. 2 standard. These craft have been extensively modified and upgraded primarily for use as command-and-control platforms for port and LOTS operations. Additional duties include personnel transfer, medical evacuation, diver support, firefighting and light salvage.

In addition to a larger and completely redesigned wheelhouse, the Mod. 2 boats feature a fully enclosed work space that takes up the aft portion of the original open cargo area. The new space is fitted with upgraded communications systems and work areas, and has a watertight hatch leading to the remaining portion of the open forward cargo bay. This area is fitted with a compact hydraulic crane and retains its opening cargo ramp, and can accommodate a Humvee or similar small vehicle, as well as salvage, diving or stevedore

U.S. Army/Steve Harding

(Left) **Having taken aboard a truck for movement to a floating causeway, an LCM-8 prepares to back away from an RRDF during a 2004 JLOTS exercise off Fort Story, Va. Just aft of the landing craft is the TSV *Spearhead*.**

(Right) **A civilian tug prepares to move two LCM-8s away from their tie-downs on the submerged main deck of the float-on/float-off cargo vessel *American Cormorant*. Also visible are three LCUs, a 128-foot tug and a third LCM-8.**

equipment. Bow pusher knees have been installed on either side of the front ramp, and each Mod. 2 is fitted with additional fendering and a firefighting monitor (water cannon).

Design of the prototype Mod. 2 (LCM-8617) began in January 1996, and conversion work on five of the vessels was done at the Army's small but capable shipyard in Hythe, England. The sixth vessel, LCM-8594, was converted at the U.S. Coast Guard Yard in Baltimore, Md. This example incorporates all of the modifications proposed for the Mod. 2, and which may not yet have been made to each of the other five craft. Current plans call for two Mod. 2s to be assigned to an active-duty floating-craft company — the 1098th Transportation Co. at Fort Eustis — and two each to the prepositioned packages in Yokohama and Europe.

At the time of writing some 72 LCM-8s, all either Mod. 1s or 2s, remained in the Army inventory. Current plans call for 24 Mod. 1s and all six Mod. 2s to remain in service through FY 2017.

U.S. Army/Steve Harding

An LCM-8 goes over the side during the 2001 download of the prepositioning ship USNS *Gopher State* at Marchwood Military Port near Southampton, England. Several LCMs are among *Gopher State's* permanent cargo, which also includes causeway sections, side-loadable warping tugs, tactical vehicles and standard commercial cargo containers.

U.S. Army/Steve Harding

Two standard Mod. 1 LCM-8s lie alongside a Mod. 2 variant at the Army watercraft facility in Hythe, England. The most obvious differences between the two vessel types are the Mod. 2's enlarged wheelhouse, the enclosed area just forward of the wheelhouse and the reduction in the size of the forward ramp.

U.S. Army/Steve Harding

U.S. Army/Steve Harding

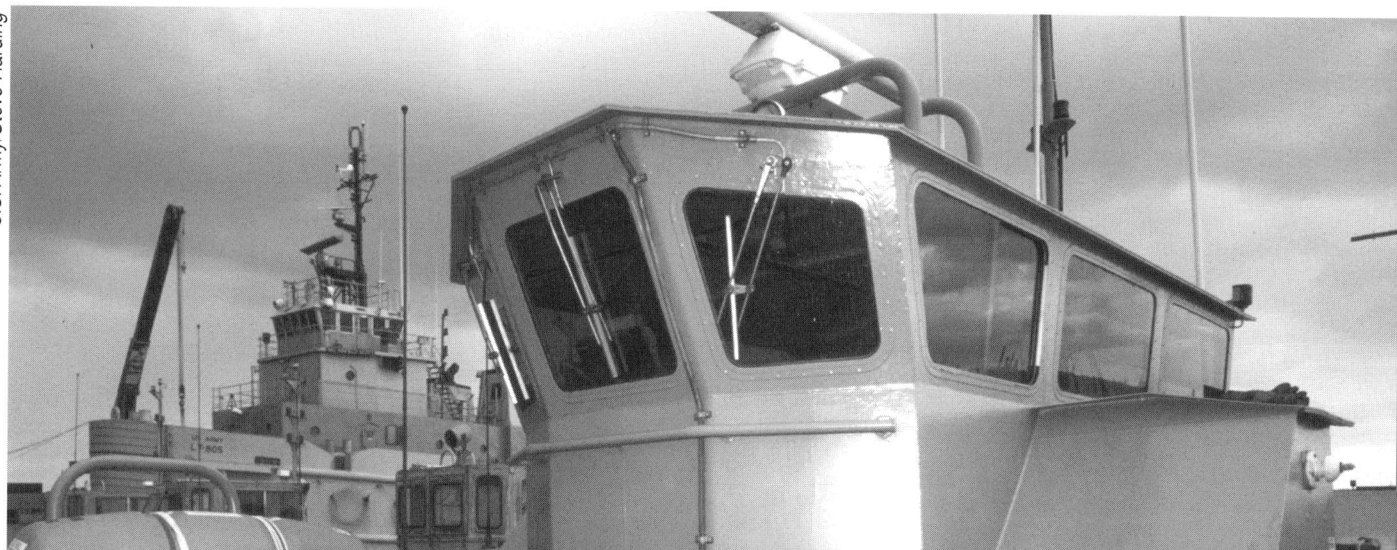

U.S. Army/Steve Harding

(Above) **The Mod. 2's fully enclosed work space takes up the aft portion of the original open cargo area. Seen here still under construction on the first prototype Mod. 2, the space is intended to house upgraded communications equipment and personnel work stations.**

(Above left) **Though reduced in area, the Mod. 2's cargo deck can still accommodate a small vehicle, as well as diving or salvage equipment. Note the pusher knees fitted to either side of the vessel's cut-down bow ramp, as well as the folded and covered hydraulic crane.**

(Left) **The Mod. 2's wheelhouse is considerably larger than that of the Mod. 1, and has been fitted with sophisticated communications and navigation systems. The pod-like device lashed down just forward of the wheelhouse is a water-pressure-activated life raft.**

Specifications

Builders:	Marinette Marine Corp., Marinette, Wis. (LCM-8500 through -8519) Gunderson Bros. Engineering Corp., Portland, Ore. (LCM-8520 through -8539) Rohr Corp., Cleves, Ohio (LCM-8540 through -8560 and 8580 through -8618)
Length overall:	74 ft.
Beam:	21 ft.
Draft:	3.5 ft (light) 5 ft. (loaded)
Displacement:	Mod. 1: 58 long tons (light) 111 long tons (loaded) Mod. 2: Not yet determined
Cargo area:	620 sq. ft. (Mods. 0/1) 206 sq. ft. (Mod. 2, approx.)
Passengers	Kwajalei: 170 Mod. 2: Up to 50
Propulsion:	Two Detroit Diesel 6-71 diesels, each generating 300 hp (400 hp per engine on SLEP vessels)
Range:	332 nm at 11 knots (light) 271 nm at 9 knots (loaded)
Crew:	6 enlisted for 24-hour operation (Mod. 1) 6 to 10, depending on mission (Mod. 2)

The LCU-1600's offset wheelhouse and fore and aft ramps give the vessel a straight-through, unencumbered cargo area that allows the speedy loading and unloading of vehicles and cargo. Thirteen vessels of this type entered Army service between 1976 and 1978.

LCU-1600

Thirteen LCU-1600-class vessels entered Army service between 1976 and 1978, primarily as replacements for the older and less capable LCU-1466-class craft. These latter boats — some 42 of which saw Army service between 1954 and the retirement of the final example in the mid-1990s — were of traditional aft-pilothouse design and had a single forward ramp. This hampered the speedy on- and off-loading of larger vehicles and containerized cargo.

This was not a problem for the Navy-designed LCU-1600-class vessels (which in Navy service are referred to as LCU-1610 class) which were built with fore and aft ramps that allow roll-on/roll-off operations. The placement of the pilot house and other main superstructure (which also contains berthing areas, a head with shower and a complete galley) to the starboard side gives the vessel a straight-through, unencumbered cargo area which allows the speedy loading of such outsized cargo as two M1 Abrams tanks or 10 double stacked, 20-foot ISO cargo containers.

A mainstay of Army watercraft operations from the time of their introduction, the LCU-1600 class vessels are intended to transport vehicles, bulk cargo and troops from ships offshore or within coastal areas and inland waters. Other tasks have included dive-team support, salvage operations, casualty evacuation and maritime drug-interdiction efforts.

The LCU-1600-class boats were key players in Army operations worldwide, and saw combat service in Panama, Somalia and the first Gulf War. Given the class's advancing age and the Army's changing watercraft requirements, however, the type is being swiftly retired. Of the 13 original examples, only three remained active at the time of writing. One (LCU-1673) serves with the Army Reserve in Washington state, a second (LCU-1675) is a harbor utility craft and training vessel at Fort Eustis, and the third fulfills a more exotic role.

Perhaps the most active of the LCU-1600-class survivors, *Manassas* (LCU-1667) belongs to the somewhat eclectic Army watercraft fleet based at Kwajalein Atoll in the Republic of the Marshall Islands. The veteran vessel is used to transport supplies, equipment, vehicles and people among the various islands that make up the Ronald Reagan Ballistic Missile Defense Test Site. Operated and maintained by the civilian contract firm that runs the mid-Pacific installation, *Manassas* is well-suited to her current job and looks set to soldier on for some time to come.

Fitted with sun awnings, LCU-1667 sits at a Kwajalein pier. *Manassas* — one of only three LCU-1600-class vessels remaining in the Army inventory — transports people equipment and supplies among the islands that make up the Ronald Reagan Ballistic Missile Test Site.

Specifications

Builders:	General Ship &Engine Works East Boston, Mass.
Length overall:	135 ft.
Beam:	29 ft.
Draft:	5.5 ft. (light) 6.6 ft. (loaded)
Displacement:	190 tons (light) 390 tons (loaded)
Cargo area:	2,103.5 sq. ft.
Propulsion:	Two General Motors 12V-71 diesels each generating 850 hp
Speed:	11 knots
Range:	1,200 nm at 12 knots (light) 1,100 nm at 11 knots (loaded)
Crew:	2 warrant officers and 12 enlisted for 24-hour operations (or 6 contractors on Kwajalein)

U.S. Army/Steve Harding

U.S. Army/Steve Harding

The LCU-2000-class vessels are of classic landing-craft design, with an aft superstructure, central open cargo area and forward ramp. At some 350 tons, the LCU's payload is equal to that carried by seven Air Force C-17 transports, and can include up to five M1 Abrams tanks.

LCU-2000

Perhaps the best indication of the value the Army places on the LCU-2000-class "landing craft, utility" is that all 35 examples of the type remain in service nearly 12 years after the delivery of the final vessel. A true jack of all trades, the LCU-2000 serves in both the active and reserve components, and has proved its worth in both peace and war.

Generally similar in layout to the larger logistics support vessel, the LCU-2000 has a forward ramp, large central cargo area and an aft superstructure. Though it does not have the LSV's aft ramp to allow drive-through loading and unloading, the vessel's 100-foot-by-36-foot open cargo area will accommodate five M1 Abrams tanks and up to 24 20-foot cargo containers. At some 350 tons, the LCU-2000's payload is equal to that carried by seven Air Force C-17 transports.

Designed specifically for Army use, the LCU-2000 provides worldwide transport of combat vehicles and sustainment cargo. Like the LSV, it also provides intratheater movement of cargo and equipment. The LCU-2000 can perform missions ranging from the roll-on/roll-off discharge of the largest Navy transport vessels to logistics-over-the-shore operations on unimproved beaches. With their relatively flat bottoms the LCU-2000s can beach and retract themselves on remote coastlines and in undeveloped or damaged port areas, an ability they have demonstrated in several of the nation's more recent armed conflicts.

U.S. Army/Steve Harding

A trainee Army mariner steers the USAV *Perryville*, LCU-2034, as the vessel's master calls out a course correction while leaving the main anchorage at Fort Eustis on a short training voyage. An LCU's compact bridge is normally occupied by no more than five people.

While the LCU-2000-class vessels can self-deploy anywhere in the world under their own power, they can also be moved as deck cargo aboard float-on/float-off and lift-on/lift-off ships. This is an especially useful characteristic, in that it allows the LCUs to be forward-stationed aboard suitable vessels, thus allowing them to arrive in a specific theater of operations much more quickly than if they'd sailed on their own from American ports.

The LCU-2000's many abilities, coupled with the fact that the average age of the fleet is just 10 years (out of a projected 25-year useful life) guarantee that it will remain a key Army asset for many years to come. Indeed, the December 2002 Army Watercraft Master Plan calls for all 35 LCU-2000s to remain in service through fiscal year 2007 — 14 based in the continental United States, 20 divided evenly between the prepositioned stocks in the Central Command and Pacific Command areas of responsibility, and one supporting the Ronald Reagan Ballistic Missile Test

U.S. Army/Steve Harding

The LCU-2000's shallow draft allows it to discharge rolling stock and other cargo directly onto a beach or pier. Here, the Kwajalein-based LCU-2021, *Great Bridge*, offloads vehicles and other cargo at the island of Roi Namur, one of several small islands that are part of the Ronald Reagan Ballistic Missile Test Site in the Marshall Islands.

A1C Thomas A. Anhalt, USAF

The LCU-2000-class vessels are also capable of carrying up to 24 standard 20-foot cargo containers, which can be loaded either through the front ramp or by crane. Here, *Five Forks* — a veteran of both Gulf wars — is seen about to get underway with a load of containers.

Site on Kwajalein Atoll in the Marshall Islands.

While the AWMP calls for the number of LCU-2000s in the fleet to drop to 20 by FY 2017 (in expectation of the acquisition and fielding of the production version of the theater support vessel), delays in or reassessments of the TSV program could well mean that more LCU-2000s remain in service over a longer period.

Given that the LCU-2000 is certain to soldier on for many more years whatever happens with

Proving that the LCU-2000-class boats will tackle any job, *Great Bridge* steams into the anchorage at Kwajalein Atoll carrying the Australian-built passenger ferry *Pvt. Sorenson* (FB-222). The new ferry's sister vessel, *Pvt. Anderson* (FB-223), also arrived in the Marshall Islands courtesy of *Great Bridge*.

the still-experimental TSV, the Army is currently exploring various improvements to the landing craft. These include structural modifications to the hull, improvement and upgrading of various mechanical systems, and extensive improvements to the LCU's communications and navigation systems. Taken together, these improvements will ensure that the LCU-2000-class vessels remain a valued part of the Army fleet for decades to come.

Specifications

Builders:	Lockheed Shipbuilding, Savannah, Ga. (LCU-2001 to 2003) Trinity-Moss Point Marine, Escatawpa, Miss. (LCU-2004 to LCU-2035)
Length overall:	174 ft.
Beam:	42 ft.
Draft:	8.5 ft.
Displacement:	672 tons (light) 1,102 tons (loaded)
Cargo area:	2,553 sq. ft.
Propulsion:	Two Cummins KTA-50M diesels, each generating 1,250 hp; twin screws with Kort nozzles
Speed:	11.5 knots
Range:	10,000 nm at 12 knots (light) 6,500 nm at 10 knots (loaded)
Crew:	2 warrant officers, 10/11 enlisted for 24-hour operations
(Note: The Kwajalein-based, contractor-operated LCU-2021 *Great Bridge* is normally operated by an 8-member civilian crew.)	

A soldier of the 7th Transportation Group guides an M1 Abrams main battle tank off an LCU and onto the sea-end of a floating causeway during a JLOTS exercise off the Virginia coast. The tank will then drive to shore — still 800 yards away — across the floating roadway.

U.S. Army/Steve Harding

U.S. Army/SPC Christina Ann Horne

An LSV at work — the *GEN Brehon B. Somervell* (LSV-3) carries vehicles of the 2nd Infantry Division through moderate seas near Pusan, South Korea. The LSV was the largest vessel type in Army service until the advent of the TSV.

LSV

The longest ships in modern Army service until the arrival of the Australian-built HSV-X1 and the even longer TSV-1X, the *GEN Frank E. Besson Jr.*-class logistics support vessels (LSVs) were, ironically, based on the design of the Singapore-built Australian roll-on/roll-off cargo vessel *Frances Bay*.

That ship — an oceangoing, ramp-equipped ro/ro vessel built to transport vehicles, cargo containers and other bulky items among the often underdeveloped ports along Australia's northern coast — had the qualities the Army was looking for in the early 1980s. At that time the service was still relying on World War II-vintage freighters for the transport of heavy or bulky cargo, which in most cases could not be landed on a beach or in an unimproved harbor. *Frances Bay*, with her relatively wide ramp, capacious cargo area and flat bottom, offered the sort of cargo capacity and beach accessibility the Army required.

The final design for the LSV drew heavily on the layout of *Frances Bay*, describing a vessel that was slightly longer and wider than the original. The LSV kept the Australian ship's long, upward-retracting bow ramp, open cargo area amidships and tall aft superstructure, but added a bow thruster for better

LSVs are capable of taking on vehicles and equipment from such larger vessels as the fast sealift ship USNS *Pollux*, shown here with the *CW3 Harold C. Clinger* (LSV-2) alongside. The LSV can also unload vehicles onto a roll-on/roll-off discharge facility, from which they can drive aboard waiting LCUs for transport to the beach.

Different fast sealift ship, same LSV. Here the *Clinger* lies alongside the USNS *Denebola* during a JLOTS operation off Fort Story, Va. In the background the *Bristoe Station* (LCU-2006) moves toward the beach. A typical JLOTS evolution includes both large naval vessels and various types of Army watercraft.

maneuverability and a stern ramp to allow through-loading of rolling stock. As designed, the LSVs could embark 24 M1 Abrams main battle tanks, up to 50 double-stacked 20-foot ISO cargo containers or up to 1,815 tons of general cargo.

The initial LSV and class namesake, *GEN Frank S. Besson Jr.*, was launched at Halter Marine's Escatawpa/Moss Point, Miss., facility in 1987. Two additional vessels followed that year, a third in 1988, a fourth in 1990 and a fifth in 1995. Five of the first six vessels were assigned to active Army units, while the sixth (LSV-3, *GEN Brehon B. Somervell*) went to the Army National Guard in Tacoma, Wash. (this unit was later transferred to the Army Reserve).

The LSV's long, upward-retracting bow ramp and capacious cargo area are well illustrated in this view, as is the type's tall aft superstructure. The LSV can embark up to 24 M1 Abrams main battle tanks or up to 50 double-stacked cargo containers, or a combination of vehicles and containers.

The self-deployable LSVs were soon busy transporting combat vehicles and sustainment cargo worldwide, moving troops and equipment along coats and rivers, and participating in logistics-over-the-shore operations. The ships proved their value and versatility in the first Gulf War, during extended operations in the Pacific and Far East, and during combat and

While vital to the LSV's ability to load and unload rolling stock, the upward-retracting bow ramp reduces forward visibility from the bridge. This shortcoming has been addressed in the design of the second-generation LSV, sometimes referred to as the Enhanced LSV.

humanitarian-aid missions in the Balkans.

As valuable to the Army as the LSVs proved themselves to be, however, they were not without their limitations. While blunt bows and flat bottoms were necessary for beach accessibility, such features also ensured relatively slow speeds, uncomfortable rides in even moderate seas and, in the case of the tall bow ramp, reduced forward visibility from the bridge. The vessels also lacked state-of-the-art communications, ship-handling and navigation systems. These shortcomings were addressed in the design of a second-generation LSV, sometimes referred to as the Enhanced LSV.

In order to improve the ship's seakeeping qualities the flat surface created by the upward-retracting tall bow ramp has been replaced in the second-generation LSV by a pointed false bow. This structure, known as

***LTG William B. Bunker* (LSV-4) approaches a berth at the port of Ash Shuaybah. LSVs have been a permanent fixture in the Persian Gulf region since the late 1990s, and continue to perform yeoman work, primarily transporting tactical vehicles and cargo containers between Kuwait and Bahrain.**

JO1 Joseph Krypel, USN

The Army's logistics support vessels played a major role in Operation Desert Storm, carrying troops and equipment throughout the theater. Here, troops muster on a pier next to *LTG William B. Bunker*, moored at the port of Ash Shuaybah.

a bow visor, can be raised upward and to the rear in order to extend the LSV's redesigned, fully articulated cargo ramp. The new 76 foot by 18 foot three-section ramp folds completely into the ship's forward hull when not in use so as not to obstruct forward visibility from the bridge. The ELSV's hull been lengthened by some 40 feet and fitted with a more bulbous forefoot to further improve seakeeping and increase speed and maneuverability. The vessel also has a more powerful bow thruster and an electric stern thruster, as well as a beach-retraction winch and twin articulating rudders.

Equally important are the less-visible changes. The second-generation LSV incorporates a state-of-the-art Litton Integrated Bridge System, which includes a voyage-management system with electronic chart display, dual Decca X- and S-band radars, an adaptive autopilot, a military P-Code Global Positioning System receiver and a weather station. Communications have also been upgraded with the addition of secure voice

***GEN Brehon B. Somervell* shows of the LSV's squared-off and businesslike stern, the most obvious features of which are the aft loading ramp and stern anchor. The latter is used primarily to help the vessel pull itself away from a beach after having landed vehicles and equipment directly ashore.**

U.S. Army/SSG David L. Pate

The LSV's rear ramp allows the roll-on/roll-off, straight-through loading of wheeled vehicles. Here, *CW3 Harold C. Clinger's* aft ramp goes down in preparation for docking with an RRDF.

and tactical VHF, UHF and HF radios, as well as a commercial satellite communications system supporting both voice and data.

A firm, fixed-price contract for the construction of the first ELSV and the option for two more was awarded to Friede Goldman Halter's Halter Marine division in May 2001. However, the parent company declared bankruptcy later that year, and its Halter Marine unit was ultimately purchased by Singapore-based ST Engg through its U.S. subsidiary, VT Systems. The renamed and reconstituted

Ramp down and secured, vehicles start rolling aboard directly from the RRDF. This type of at-sea ramp loading can also be done from watercraft to watercraft.

U.S. Army/SSG David L. Pate

VT Halter Marine continued work on the first ELSV, which was launched in May 2003 as *SSG Robert T. Kuroda* (LSV-7). The keel of LSV-8 was laid two months earlier and the vessel, christened *MG Robert Smalls*, was launched in April 2004.

The December 2002 Army Watercraft Master Plan calls for eight LSVs to remain active through fiscal year 2013, when the number will drop to seven (and then to six in FY 2015). Two of the vessels are to be homeported in the continental United States (LSV-4 at Fort Eustis and LSV-8 in Baltimore, Md.), while the others are to be forward-stationed (LSV-1 in Kuwait, LSV-6 in Europe, and LSVs 2, 5 and 7 in Hawaii).

However, the ultimate size and basing of the Army's fleet of logistics support vessels will ultimately depend in large part on the as-yet-undetermined fate of the theater support vessel. The number of TSVs the Army puts into service, and where they're based, will determine the LSV's final disposition. Despite the uncertainty, it is safe to assume that some number of LSVs will remain in Army service for the foreseeable future.

The LSV's cavernous main cargo area can hold a variety of vehicles, from trucks and trailers to tanks and helicopters (when their blades are folded). Here, *CW3 Harold C. Clinger* embarks rolling stock belonging to the 2nd Infantry Division.

U.S. Army/Benny Moritz

Loaded with cargo of a different kind — construction equipment and humanitarian-relief supplies — *SP4 James A. Loux* (LSV-6) prepares to leave Fort Eustis bound for Kosovo.

Her ramp partially down, *CW3 Harold C. Clinger* prepares to put her load of vehicles ashore at Pusan, Korea. Crew members stand ready to ground-guide the trucks and Humvees safely onto the pier.

MG Charles P. Gross forges ahead in this fine underway study. Note, however, that her blunt bow is kicking up a considerab swell ahead of the vessel, a factor that both slows the ship and makes for an uncomfortable ride in even moderate seas. Th design of the Enhanced LSV is intended to fix this shortcoming.

VT Halter Marine, Inc.

SSG Robert T. Kuroda (LSV-7), the first of two currently funded ELSVs, slides down the ways in May 2003. The second ELS *MG Robert Smalls* (LSV-8), was launched in April 2004. The two new vessels incorporate a host of new electronics, including state-of-the-art Litton Integrated Bridge System and secure VHF, UHF and HF radios.

Specifications

(Both versions, unless otherwise noted)

Builders:	Halter-Moss Point Marine, Escatawpa, Miss. (LSVs 1-6) VT Halter Marine, Escatawpa, Miss. (LSVs 7 & 8)
Length overall:	272 ft. (1-6) 314 ft. (7 & 8)
Beam:	60 ft.
Draft:	12 ft.
Displacement:	1,612 tons (light) (1-6) 4,199 tons (loaded) (1-6) (Not yet determined for 7 & 8)
Cargo area:	10,500 sq. ft.
Propulsion:	Two General Motors EMD 16-645-E2 diesels (1-6) Two caterpillar 3561B diesels (7 & 8)
Speed:	10 knots (1-6) 12 knots (7 & 8)
Range:	8,200 nm at 12.5 knots (light) 6,500 nm at 11.5 knots (loaded) (Not yet determined for 7 & 8)
Crew:	8 warrant officers and 24 enlisted for 24-hour operations

SSG Robert T. Kuroda shows off her redesigned bow. The square structure just aft of her stem is the articulated bow ramp, shown in the folded position. LSV-7 will join the Army Reserve's 9th Regional Support Command in Honolulu, Hawaii, (already home to two active-duty LSVs) while LSV-8 will join the 99th Regional Readiness Cmd. in Baltimore, Md.

VT Halter Marine, Inc.

The Modular Causeway System allows vehicles and other cargo to be off-loaded at sea from a cargo ship, either drive directly aboard the causeway ferry via the Roll-On/Roll-Off Discharge Facility or lowered by crane. Here, some vehicles ar already aboard the CF that will take them ashore, while others await transportation.

MODULAR CAUSEWAY SYSTEM

Given that one of the primary purposes of Army watercraft is to get vehicles and equipment from ship to shore when deep-water port facilities are unavailable or unusable, the role played by the Modular Causeway System, or MCS, is a vital one.

Simply put, the MCS consists of interchangeable watertight, welded-steel pontoon sections of various sizes and shapes, some powered and some unpowered, each of which can be transported as deck or internal cargo on military or commercial cargo ships.

Once in the area of operations the MCS sections can be assembled into four configurations — the Roll-On/Roll-Off Discharge Facility, the Causeway Ferry, the Floating Causeway and the Side-Loadable Warping Tug. Each of the individual configurations plays a specific role in the Joint Logistics Over the Shore (JLOTS) operations that move vehicles and cargo from a vessel lying offshore to the beach.

Roll-On/Roll-Off Discharge Facility (RRDF)

Essentially an offshore pier secured lengthwise alongside a military or commercial roll-on/roll-off (RORO) vessel, the RRDF is made up of unpowered MCS pontoon sections secured to one another usin male and female connecters built into each sectior The RRDF is comprised of the RORO section, whic is usually about 65 feet wide and 180 feet long; a offloading ramp that runs from the RORO ship's hu opening to the level of the RRDF; and a platforn fendering system.

Once the RRDF has been assembled alongsid the offshore vessel, vehicles can simply drive down th ramp from the ship and onto the RRDF. There they ar maneuvered into position to be backed up the lowere ramps of waiting LCUs or LCMs, or onto causewa ferries, which then transport the vehicles to the beac or to the floating causeway. The RRDF can also b used to load standard shipboard cargo container aboard waiting watercraft, though this is normally don by simply winching the containers off the ship's deck an lowering them directly onto the smaller craft.

Causeway Ferry (CF)

The CF consists of two powered MCS section aft (one bearing a rudimentary pilothouse), two o more unpowered intermediate sections in the cente and two sloped front-end sections that allow vehicles to be driven off the CF onto the shore or a floating causeway. Vehicles can be driven directly aboard the CF at the RRDF, or they and other types of cargo can be lowered aboard by crane.

Floating Causeway (FC)

The FC is made up of unpowered MCS pontoon sections joined together lengthwise to form a temporary floating pier with one end anchored on the beach and the other projecting up to 900 feet offshore. On the seaward end of the FC (and often on either side as well) are MCS sections with ramped ends that allow vehicles to be driven off landing craft or causeway ferries directly onto the FC, from where they are then driven to shore.

The FC is essential to JLOTS operations when the beach gradient does not allow ramp-equipped landing craft such as LCU-2000s or LCM-8s to discharge vehicles directly ashore.

U.S. Army/Steve Harding

(*Right*) A side-loadable warping tug is off-loaded from the USNS *Gopher State* during an exercise. The SLWT looks much like a short causeway ferry, and is assembled from two powered sections attached astern of several unpowered sections.

(*Below*) A causeway ferry heads for the beach with a load of vehicles. The CF consists of two powered MCS sections aft, two or more unpowered intermediate sections in the center and two sloped front-end sections. A rudimentary pilothouse is set to the starboard side aft.

Side Loadable Warping Tug (SLWT)

Looking much like a shortened causeway ferry, the SLWT is assembled from two powered MCS sections attached astern of several unpowered sections. Though the barge-like SLWT is ungainly looking — it's 85 feet long, rectangular, low in the water and has a small pilothouse set off to one side — the swiveling heads on its two water-jet propulsion units make it more maneuverable than it looks. That's a plus, because the craft's job is to assemble and tend both the RRDF and the FC. It also tends the anchors of both structures, and can be pressed into service to move light cargo on its own.

In 1989 and 1992 the Army awarded contracts that ultimately resulted in the construction of two RRDFs, five CFs, two FCs and five SLWTs. In 2001 a further contract was let for two additional RRDFs, one FC and two SLWTs. The 2002 Army Watercraft Master

***(Left)* The causeway ferry is capable of moving a considerable number of vehicles ashore on each trip, depending on the size and weight of the vehicles transported. It can also carry standard cargo containers, pallets and helicopters.**

***(Below)* Causeway ferries can discharge their cargos of vehicles directly onto the floating causeway, from where they can simply drive to shore. Here, an M1 Abrams main battle tank heads for the beach, with a little help from soldiers acting as ground guides.**

U.S. Army/Steve Harding

U.S. Army/Steve Harding

Side-loadable warping tugs embarked as deck cargo aboard the prepositioning ship USNS *Gopher State* can be operational within minutes of hitting the water. Their primary task is to aid in the assembly of the floating causeway, and then husband it once it is operational.

Plan envisions a need for eight RRDFs, six CFs and six FCs, all to be equally divided between one active and one Reserve causeway company. All of the current MCS assets belong to the 7th Transportation Group at Fort Eustis, though much of the equipment is actually prepositioned aboard fast sealift ships or in storage areas ashore.

Specifications

Roll-On/Roll-Off Discharge Facility:

Builders:	Robishhaw Engineering, Houston, Texas Lakeshore Inc., Iron Mountain, Mich.

Causeway section (intermediate) length: beam: depth:	80 ft. 24 ft. 4 ft.
Causeway section (beach/sea end) length: beam: depth:	85 ft. 24 ft. 4.5 ft.
Calm water ramp length:	120 ft.

Causeway Ferry and Floating Causeway:

MCS sections are the same dimensions as intermediate and beach/sea end sections of the RRDF.

The CF's powered section is made up of two propulsion modules, each eight feet wide and 40 feet long, and an unpowered center module. The propulsion

U.S. Army/Steve Harding

A side-loadable warping tug maneuvers in Southampton Water during a causeway exercise held near the Army's watercraft facility in Hythe, England. The SLWT is an ungainly looking craft, but its waterjet propulsion system makes it far more maneuverable than it looks.

U.S. Army/Steve Harding

The SLWT nudges a causeway section toward two already connected sections, as soldiers stand ready with the picks and sledge hammers used to join the opposing sections' male and female connectors. One locked in place, the connectors keep the sections firmly joined despite wave action and the weight of vehicles using the causeway.

A causeway ferry moves slowly toward a fast sealift ship. The fence-like devices on the vessel's bow are fold-out roadway sections that are deployed when the CF docks — bow on — to the RRDF or floating causeway.

is provided by two eight cylinder, 600hp marine diesels driving 5,000-pound output steerable pump jets.

Side Loadable Warping Tug:

Length:	85 ft.
Beam:	21 ft.
Draft:	5 ft.
Powerplant:	Two GM8V71TI marine diesels, each producing 450hp, driving two steerable 30,000 gallon-per-minute hydrojets.
Crew:	Six enlisted soldiers.

SMALL TUG (900)

Built to a design by Corning Townsend of Connecticut-based C.T. Marine, the shallow-draft ST-900-class boats have twice the towing capacity of the earlier 65-foot small tugs and are intended to tow and husband general-cargo barges in harbors, inland waterways and along coastlines. The ST-900 can also assist larger tugs with such general utility work as docking and undocking ships of all sizes, moving floating cranes and line-handling. The tug is fitted with push knees to enable it to better move barges within congested ports and waterways.

The ST-900's compact size allows it to be easily transportable as deck cargo on larger vessels. Indeed, current planning calls for two ST-900s to be assigned to each floating craft company, which also includ one large tug and a 115-ton barge derrick. In tests a Tacoma, Wash., the 115-ton BD of the Army Reserve' 467th Transportation Company lifted both of the unit' small tugs (ST-905 and ST-906) onto its own forwar deck. The idea was that the unit's large tug could to the BD, which in turn would carry the small tugs.

The ST-900 is capable of operation in Sea Stat 3, and able to operate in Sea State 2 when fully loade with no tow. It has a maximum range of 720 nautic miles, and is capable of up to 120 hours of continuou operation. The boat has one single and one triple cabi with a small galley and shower-equipped head, as we as a dinette with seating for four.

U.S. Army/Terry Lauscher

The past and the present share pier space at Fort Eustis — the ST-900-class tug *Appomattox* (ST-907) seems to tower over the 1950s-built 100-foot tug *Champagne-Marne* (LT-1974). This photo well illustrates the new type's compact shape, which allows it to be easily transportable as deck cargo on larger vessels.

U.S. Army/Terry Lauscher

The small tug dispatched to Kuwait to participate in Operation Iraqi Freedom did yeoman service, and was kept so busy that it went through several times the amount of fuel that was initially forecast for the mission.

The Army has identified a need for 16 examples of the ST-900, with 15 funded as of May 2003.

The ST-900-class tugs are fitted with push knees — clearly visible in this photo of *Pelham Point* (ST-902) — to enable them to better move barges within congested ports and waterways. The vessel immediately aft of the small tug is the 128-foot large tug *COL Seth Warner* (LT-806).

U.S. Army/Steve Harding

Fort Stanwix (ST-903) moves slowly past anchored LCUs at Fort Eustis. The ST-900-class boats are extremely maneuverable and are operated by a single person sitting in the narrow wheelhouse. The circular device in the center of the forward window provides a clear outside view even in driving rain or heavy seas.

U.S. Army/Terry Lauscher

Soldiers use guidelines to ensure *Pelham Point* comes aboard safely while being loaded onto the forward deck of a 115-ton barge derrick. Current plans call for two ST-900s to be assigned to each floating craft company, which also will include a BD and a 128-foot large tug. The STs can be deployed aboard the BD, which will itself be moved by the LT.

Specifications

Builders:	Orange Shipbuilding, Orange, Texas
Length overall:	60 ft.
Beam:	22 ft.
Draft:	6 ft.
Displacement:	110 tons
Main propulsion:	Two Cummins KTA19-M3 diesels, each rated at 640hp.

Service speed:	10 knots
Bollard pull:	30,000 lbs. (ahead), 15,000 lbs. (astern) and 4,000 lbs. (sideways)
Range:	720 nm at 6 knots (light) Range with tow is variable.
Crew:	2 warrant officers, 10 enlisted for 24-hour operations.

U.S. Army/Steve Harding

Quite powerful for their size, the ST-900 boats are also capable of husbanding large vessels. Here, *Fort Stanwix* moves into position alongside *SP4 James A. Loux* (LSV-6) during a training session at Fort Eustis.

Valley Forge (LT-2096) shows off the 100-foot large tug's classic lines. Designed and built in the 1950s, the four remaining 100-foot LTs are the survivors of 65 examples that formed the backbone of the Army's tug fleet for several decades. Rugged and dependable, the 100-footers were capable of self-deploying virtually anywhere in the world.

LARGE TUG (100 ft.)

Though slated to completely disappear from the inventory by the end of fiscal year 2005, the 100-foot large tug was for decades the workhorse of the Army's watercraft fleet and remains, at least in the minds of many Army mariners both past and present, the quintessential Army tugboat.

Officially known as Design 3006, the 100-foot tug is of standard layout — wheelhouse well forward atop an elongated superstructure, exhaust stack immediately aft of the wheelhouse, and a broad deck sloping from a high stem to a broad counter stern. Sixty-five examples were built by several yards during the early 1950s, and the design proved rugged and dependable under virtually all conditions — as indicated by the fact that in the late 1950s three of the tugs self-deployed from New Orleans to Yokohama, Japan.

The 100-foot tug has served in every conflict and every theater in which the Army has been active since the end of the Korean War, including the most recent war with Iraq. Indeed, one of the last four examples of the type remaining in Army service, LT-1974, did yeoman duty in and around Kuwaiti

A 100-foot tug moves slowly through the heavily damaged Kuwaiti port of Ash Shuyabah soon after its recapture from Iraqi forces during Operation Desert Storm. The tugs did yeoman work during that conflict both in the war zone and in Stateside ports.

The 100-foot tug has seen service in every theater and conflict since the end of the Korean War, including the most recent war with Iraq. Indeed, the vessel shown here, LT-1974, performed a range of vital missions in and around Kuwaiti ports during that conflict. She and her crew were even commended by the Navy for the support they provided that service during the war.

With all monitors in operation, *Valley Forge* demonstrates her firefighting capabilities during an exercise at Sunny Point Military Ocean Terminal in North Carolina. A four-year overhaul and modernization at the Army's shipyard facility in England made LT-2096 possibly the most technologically advanced of the remaining 100-footers.

ports during the latter conflict. In an interesting twist, its crew was awarded the Navy and Marine Corps Commendation medal for actions in support of naval special-warfare forces. Indeed, the vessel was slated to remain on duty in Kuwait until the late-2004 arrival of one of the newly rebuilt 128-foot tugs.

One reason for the 100-footer's longevity has been an aggressive program of modernization and modification. These periodic improvement programs — known as "flights" I, II and III — have included both ongoing upgrades of the vessel's basic systems and more extensive changes intended to broaden the vessel's capabilities in such important areas as firefighting. The former include the replacement of the original 1,200 hp diesel engine by a 2,150 hp or 2,600 hp unit, the addition of Kort nozzels around the screw, newer communications and navigation systems, upgraded crew berthing and mess facilities, and differing deck equipment. The latter have included the installation of modern fire monitors and related systems on those vessels tapped to serve as dedicated firetugs.

Possibly the most technologically advanced of the four 100-footers remaining in Army service at the time of writing is *Valley Forge*, LT-2096. Built in 1954 by National Steel and Shipbuilding in San Diego, Calif., the contractor-crewed tug is assigned to the Army's 597th Transportation Terminal Group. *Valley Forge's* primary mission is to serve as a firefighting vessel at the Sunny Point Military Ocean Terminal in Southport, N.C., and it is a task for which the boat has been well equipped.

A four-year overhaul and modernization at the Army's European shipyard in Hythe, England, gave LT-2096 a more powerful engine, a bow thruster, state-of-the-art communication and navigation systems, and the most

U.S. Army/Steve Harding

Solidly braced, a 100-foot tug undergoes overhaul and conversion at Hythe. The most obvious addition to the tug is the Kort nozzle surrounding the single screw. The nozzle helps move more water past the screw at a higher speed, helping to create more thrust for the same input power and torque.

Looking ready for anything, *Champagne-Marne* shows off some of the other additions made to the 100-footers during their overhauls at Hythe. Most notable are the additional fire monitors — two were added aft of the stack on either side of the superstructure, with a third just above and aft of the wheelhouse.

modern and extensive firefighting systems available.

Valley Forge's firefighting equipment was put to the test in the most spectacular way on July 14, 2001, when a fire broke out aboard the 950-foot-long ammunition ship MV *Carter*, then loading a Kuwait-bound cargo at Sunny Point. The tug's crew was able to keep a steady stream of cooling water on the burning ship, preventing the spread of the flames and the possible detonation of her cargo.

Over the course of its service life the 100-foot tug has undertaken such missions as berthing and unberthing large cargo vessels; inland waterway, coastal and open-ocean towing; firefighting; salvage; diver support; and general utility work. Though self-deployable depending on sea state, distance and crew training, the 100-foot tug is normally deployed as deck cargo aboard float-on/float-off vessels. Indeed, the 100-footer was standard cargo for the prepostioning vessel *American Cormorant* for the length of that ship's Army contract.

Valley Forge's **exterior modifications — including upgraded fire monitors, modified deck arrangement, increased bow fendering and more extensive antenna arrays — are readily apparent when the vessel is compared to the less-modified 100-footer to her right.**

U.S. Army/Steve Harding

The 100-foot tugs were standard cargo aboard the prepositioning vessel *American Cormorant* until after the first Gulf War. Here, three of the tugs (including LT-2081 and LT-1960, both now retired) are about to be towed off the semi-submerged cargo vessel by the British commercial tug *Wyetow* during a download undertaken in Southampton Water.

Specifications

Builders:	Avondale Marine Ways, West Wego, La. (LT-1936 through -1964) Higgins, Inc., New Orleans, La. (LT-1965 through -1977, and LT-2088) National Steel and Shipbuilding, San Diego, Calif. (LT-2075 through -2087) Matton Shipyard, Cohoes, N.Y. (LT-2095 and possibly others)
Length overall:	107 ft.
Beam:	27 ft.
Draft:	8 ft. 10 in. (light) 12.5 ft. (loaded)
Displacement:	295 long tons (light) 390 long tons (loaded)
Propulsion:	One Fairbanks Morse 37F16 diesel generating 1,200 hp (Flight I) One Cooper-Bessimer diesel generating 1,200 hp (Flight II) One EMD 12-645 diesel generating 2,150 hp (Flight III) One 2,500 diesel (LT-2096)
Bollard pull:	32 tons
Speed:	12.75 knots (light)
Range:	3,323 nm (light)
Crew:	6-8

Though now virtually extinct in Army service, the 100-foot tug is still considered by many Army mariners to be the most capable tug the service has ever had.

FLOATING UTILITY CRAFT

LARGE TUG (128 ft.)

In 1988 the Navy, acting on the Army's behalf, awarded a contract to the New York-based Robert E. Derecktor firm for the first new oceangoing tugboat to be acquired by the Army in some 40 years.

The new vessel was intended for coastal and ocean towing, and docking and undocking operations with large ocean vessels. It was also meant to be capable of providing limited firefighting, salvage and rescue assistance to other vessels and shore installations. In short, the new large tug (LT) was supposed to outperform in all respects the remaining examples of the 100-foot large tug (Design 3006) still in the inventory.

The early drawings for the new LT were based to some extent on that of *Chevron Star*, a smaller harbor tug designed some years earlier by the well-known naval architects Al and Joe Hack of Long Island, N.Y. The Army felt that, despite her smaller size, *Chevron Star's* hull shape and transverse framing suited the rather stringent requirements the service had in mind.

While initial concept drawings for the new LT envisioned a vessel of about 148 feet, during the actual design process this was shortened to 128 feet in

Based in part on a commercial tug design, the 128-foot tug was intended for coastal and open-ocean towing, as well as handling large ocean-going vessels. However, the decision to shorten the vessel from 148 feet to 128 feet, while retaining her tall superstructure, caused serious stability problems.

U.S. Army/Terry Lauscher

U.S. Army/Terry Lauscher

an attempt to make the new LT more maneuverable within small or congested harbors. The vessel's height was not similarly reduced, however, and the design change was to have unforeseen and undesirable consequences.

Derecktor began construction of the hulls of the first six vessels of a projected eight-ship class at its Middletown, R.I., yard. By the time of the firm's 1991 bankruptcy, workers had essentially completed the hulls of the first two vessels, about 90 percent of the third and approximately 30 percent on the fourth. Completion of the existing hulls and construction of two further examples was ultimately undertaken by Trinity/Halter Marine's Moss Point, Miss., yard, which

This view of *the* 01 and 02 levels on *COL Seth Warner* (LT-806) well illustrates the tall, narrow nature of the original design's superstructure. The 02 level (just below the wheelhouse) housed the tug's radio room, arms room, damage-control center and medical locker.

This view of *MG Anthony Wayne* (LT-803), the first of the large tugs to be converted, shows the lower, larger wheelhouse to good advantage. Current plans call for the rebuilding of the five remaining LTs to be completed by the end of fiscal year 2007.

MG Anthony Wayne **lies alongside at Hythe before her conversion began. In addition to lowering and reconfiguring the vessel's wheelhouse, the conversion also lowered her funnels, added more extensive fendering, reconfigured the H-bitt and added a range of new electronics.**

was held harmless on the craft's flawed design. All six vessels were completed in 1994, though construction of the final two examples was ultimately cancelled.

One of the first three examples of the 128-foot LT underwent performance testing with the 73rd Transportation Company at Fort Eustis, while the other two went to the Army Reserve's 949th Trans. Co. in Baltimore, Md.

One of the latter vessels, *MG Henry Knox*, later made a record Army peacetime voyage when it towed the unmanned 100-foot tug *Normandy* from Baltimore to Tacoma, Wash., for delivery to the Army Reserve's 497th Trans. Co. The passage from Maryland to the Panama Canal took a week, with *Normandy* on a stern tow. Once at the canal the older tug was reconfigured to a hip tow on *MG Henry Knox's* port side, and the canal transit from the Atlantic side to the Miraflores Locks took 14 hours. The last leg of the voyage to Tacoma took 15 days.

While it was a tremendous accomplishment, the *MG Henry Knox's* coast-to-coast voyage also highlighted the continuing stability problems inherent in the LT's design. Shortening the vessel's hull without reducing the height of its superstructure kept the tug's vertical center of gravity high, making it potentially unstable in even moderate seas. In heavy seas, or on extended transoceanic passages, this became a serious issue, in that even seasoned Army mariners were made seasick by the ship's very poor seakeeping.

And there were other problems, too. Crews of the LTs soon discovered that the vessel's fendering was inadequate and unsafe, and that noise levels on the decks between and directly aft of the twin funnels were far beyond safe or acceptable limits. Moreover, there were problems with the LT's fuel tanks; the layout of the pilothouse was inefficient and precluded the installation of upgraded electronics; and the design of the H-bitt — the large metal device mounted just aft of the tow winch that was intended to keep towlines from pulling the tug too far to either side — was inefficient.

Since the LT was intended to become the Army's sole large tug for line units, correcting these many problems became an absolute necessity. In 1998 the British marine engineering firm International Consultants Inc. (ICI) won a contract for the redesign of the tug's fuel-transfer system. And in February

2002 ICI, which is headquartered near the Army's small shipyard at Hythe, was tapped to undertake a comprehensive redesign and re-engineering of the LT.

ICI's plan for the revamped LT calls for the complete removal of the structure on the tug's 02 level — which in the original configuration houses the radio room, arms room, damage-control center and medical locker — and installing on that level a pilothouse that is lower, wider and longer than the current version. In addition, the tug's funnels will be lowered, better and more extensive fendering will be added, the aft H-bitt will be reconfigured, and cabling will be installed for upgraded electronic systems in the pilothouse. Taken together, these changes are intended to lower the vessel's vertical center of gravity (and thus significantly increase its stability) while also making it a more modern and more capable ocean-going military tug.

Work on the first vessel to be reconfigured (LT-803) began at Hythe early in 2003. Current plans call for the rebuilding of the five remaining LTs to be completed by the end of fiscal year 2007. Hulls LT-801 and 805 arrived in Hythe in January 2004 from Yokohama, Japan, to begin their upgrades, while LT-804 reached England four months later.

As originally built the 128-ft large tug generates 50 tons of bollard pull, allowing it to tow five Type 231A or 231B barges (which see), or the 115-ton barge derrick, and the tug can sustain a minimum speed of 5 knots in Sea State 4 when under full tow. What effects the type's redesign will have on vessel performance is unclear, though projections suggest performance will improve considerably across the board.

The Army Watercraft Master Plan calls for each floating craft company (one active, one Reserve) to receive a single LT, and for two vessels to go to each of the two prepositioning sites. Given that the type's minimum service life was estimated at 25 years even before the rebuild, the LT seems set to remain in the Army inventory well into the future.

Even before conversion, the LT's wheelhouse was well laid out in terms of placement of controls and communications and navigation equipment. However, even in this photo the structure's great height above the waterline is readily apparent by looking at the pier-side buildings.

U.S. Army/Steve Harding

The Army's largest and smallest tugs are shown together in this view of the January 2004 download of the *American Cormorant* in Southampton Water. The small tug *Dorchester Heights* (ST-901) moves *MG Nathanael Greene* (LT-801) away from her deck moorings before towing her to Hythe. The other tug visible in this shot is the Navy yard tug YTB-834.

Specifications
(Original Design)

Builders:	Robert E. Derecktor, Middleton, R.I. (initial contract) Trinity/Halter Marine, Moss Point, Miss.
Length overall:	128 ft., 4 in.
Beam:	36 ft.
Draft:	14.5 ft. (light) 16 ft. 10 in. (loaded)
Displacement:	786 long tons (light) 1,057 long tons (loaded)

Main propulsion:	Two GM EMD 645 F7B diesels, each generating 1,700hp
Fuel consumption:	168 gph
Speed:	Variable, depending on tow
Bollard pull:	50 long tons
Range:	5,000 nm at 13.5 knots (light) 5,000 nm at 12 knots (loaded)
Crew:	8 warrant officers, 15 enlisted for 24-hour operations.

Kwajalein Tugs

Throughout the history of Army watercraft operations there have been occasions when the service has acquired one or two examples of a nonstandard vessel to fill a very specific need. Such was the case in late 1986 when the Army leased two oceangoing tugboats for use on Kwajalein Atoll.

Located some 2,500 miles southeast of Hawaii in the Marshall Islands, the atoll is a necklace-shaped string of small islets dispersed over 1,100 square miles of ocean and encompassing the world's largest lagoon. The United States has maintained a military outpost on Kwajalein since capturing it the from the Japanese in 1944, and over the past two decades the atoll has become a key American missile-testing facility.

While Navy tugboats had been assigned to Kwajalein even after operations on the atoll were taken over by the Army in 1964, by the mid-1980s it became apparent that the Army would need its own vessels in order to deal with the ever-increasing tempo of missile-testing operations. The tugs would have to be able to dock and undock large vessels, undertake open-ocean towing, provide supplemental firefighting and salvage support, and self-deploy to Hawaii, Australia and other destinations in the Pacific as required.

While the Army's then-standard 100-foot tug (Design 3006) was capable of fulfilling these requirements, the type's age and growing scarcity in the fleet convinced the U.S. Army Strategic Defense Command to look at other alternatives. A survey of modern oceangoing tugs capable of fulfilling the Army's requirements gave planners a good idea of the type and size of vessel they needed, and they found two likely candidates in *Gulf Condor* and *Gulf Raven*.

Built in Louisiana in 1981 for Gulf Fleet Equipment Company, the two tugs were of a twin-

Mystic shows off her classic lines while alongside at Kwajalein. The vessel and her sister _Gulf Condor_ were built in 1981 for Gulf Fleet Equipment Company, and were leased in 1987. They made the long passage from Louisiana to the Marshall Islands under their own power.

U.S. Army/Steve Harding

screw design then popular for commercial open-ocean work. At 120 feet and 193 tons they were considered to be of medium size, a characteristic that Army planners felt would allow the vessels to work well both within the harbor at Kwajalein Island and in the open waters of the lagoon and surrounding ocean.

Gulf Condor and *Gulf Raven* were initially leased from Zapata Gulf Marine Operators, a subsidiary of Gulf Fleet Equipment Co., and voyaged from the United States to Kwajalein in July 1987 under their own power. This feat was made even more impressive by the fact that the tugs towed a 160-foot-long Army cargo barge (BG-184) on the passage to Kwajalein.

The tugs were put to work soon after their arrival, and proved so well-suited to duty on Kwajalein that the Army exercised the purchase option in the lease contract with Zapata Marine Operators. Once *Gulf Condor* and *Gulf Raven* officially belonged to the Army they were christened LT-101 and LT-102, respectively, and eventually renamed USAV *Gulf Condor* and USAV *Mystic*[1].

In the years since their arrival on Kwajalein the tugs have done yeoman duty, with an occasional break for drydocking in Australia. The Army currently has no plans to replace Gulf Condor and Mystic, so they seem set for many more years of service at America's outpost in the Marshall Islands.

Gulf Condor lies near the largest vessel in the Kwajalein "fleet," the range safety vessel *Worthy*. After this photo was taken both LT-101 and LT-102 were repainted gray overall, though *Worthy* retains her white scheme to make her more visible to test aircraft and other vessels.

Specifications

Builders:	Quality Shipyards, Houma, La.
Length overall:	120 ft. 11 in.
Beam:	34 ft.
Draft:	14 ft.
Displacement:	193 tons
Propulsion:	Twin EMD 12-645-E6 diesels, producing 4,200hp and driving twin screws.
Speed:	12 knots (light) 6 knots (heavy)
Range:	8,800 nm
Crew:	7

U.S. Army/Steve Harding

[1] These nonstandard names and the tugs' out-of-sequence hull numbers reflect their unique status within the Army watercraft fleet. All of the Army vessels on Kwajalein operate on what's known as a "Table of Distribution and Allowances" (TDA) status, meaning that they are not assigned to doctrinally defined operational field units (such as heavy-boat companies), but rather to nontactical, infrastructure-support organizations. *Gulf Condor* and *Mystic* "belong" to the U.S. Army Space and Missile Defense Command, and the vessels' operation and maintenance are SMDC's responsibility. Like all the vessels in Kwajalein's "fleet," LT-101 and LT-102 are operated by civilian contract crews.

Fairly compact, the 100-ton barge derricks are easily transportable aboard semi-submersible vessels.

BARGE DERRICKS
(100 AND 115 TON)

While admittedly not the most esthetically pleasing vessels ever built, the utilitarian barge derricks (more commonly referred to as floating cranes) are an indispensable part of the Army's watercraft fleet. Built expressly to transfer heavy and outsize cargoes from fast sealift ships to smaller vessels, or from those vessels onto piers, the unpowered floating cranes can be towed overseas or, in the case of the earlier 100-ton version, can be deck-loaded aboard a semi-submersible ship for transport.

There are currently two examples of the earlier 100-ton floating crane (Design BD-264B) remaining in the inventory, *Naples* and *Big Bethel*. The former is homeported at Fort Eustis, and the latter at Hythe, England. Built in the early 1950s, the two vessels were extensively refurbished between 1996 and 1998 to both improve their lifting capability and enhance the berthing facilities for their crews.

Each 100-ton floating crane is mounted on the aft end of a rigid, welded-steel barge. The main hoist has a maximum rated-left capacity of 200,000 pounds or 100 short tons, while the auxiliary lift has a maximum rated capacity of 56,000 pounds or 28 short tons. The crane can rotate a full 360 degrees, and has two power systems — direct-current generators that powers the crane's hoisting and rotating equipment, and alternating-current generators that provide for electric lighting and other ship's services.

Although the 100-ton floating cranes must be towed or carried to their work sites, they are self-

U.S. Army/Steve Harding

sustaining once on-site and are intended to house their crews for extended periods of time. They are thus fitted with air-conditioned, six-bunk berthing areas and upgraded sanitation facilities. Their galleys have electric ranges, large refrigerators, fresh-water tanks and a small dining area. The radio-equipped crane-operator's station is also air-conditioned.

As useful as the BD-264B floating cranes have been during their service lives, they've long suffered from two serious shortcomings. First, they are unable to lift the M1A1 Abrams tank and, second, their booms are not long enough to reach to the top decks of the newest Navy fast sealift ships.

The remedy for those shortcomings is a new vessel, the 115-ton BD. It is the first new class of floating crane built for the Army in 40 years, and is intended to be capable of loading and unloading existing and projected shipping through the year 2020. The vessel has a secondary mission of conducting salvage missions and clearing debris from ports and inland waterways.

The BD 115 is transportable aboard float-on/float-off ships. It is unpowered, and is towed into position and husbanded by a 128-foot large tug.

The BD 115's marine crane is capable of lifting 115 long tons at 175 feet, which allows it to lift and

Much larger than its 100-ton predecessor, the 115-ton BD has a main hoist capable of lifting M1 tanks from the top decks of the largest Navy cargo ships. This view of *Delaware* (BD-6804) well illustrates the size of the main hoist.

discharge M1A1/M1A2 Abrams tanks from the uppermost deck of the Navy's largest roll-on/roll-off cargo ship. In addition to the 115-ton main hoist, the crane has a 25-long ton auxiliary hoist and 5-long ton whip hoist. Hydraulic power is supplied by a 1,200 hp diesel engine.

Because it is intended for 24-hour operations, the BD 115 is equipped with berthing for its 15-member crew, as well as washrooms, a galley, a mess hall, a small medical facility and a laundry.

The first vessel in the class, *Keystone State*, was so named in honor of the 13 members of the Army Reserve's Pennyslvania-based 14th Quartermaster Detachment killed by a 1991 Iraqi Scud missile attack on Dhahran, Saudi Arabia, during Operation Desert Storm.

The 2002 Army Watercraft Master Plan cites a need for five examples of the BD 115, one each for four active Army floating-craft companies, and a fifth for an Army Reserve company. Four vessels have so far been delivered, and funding for a fifth was pending at press time.

Specifications

100-Ton

Builders:	Dravo Corp., Pittsburgh, Pa.
Length overall:	140 ft.
Beam:	70 ft.
Draft:	6 ft. 3 1/4 in. (full load)
Displacement:	1,630 long tons (full load)
Boom length:	123 ft. 6 in.
Main block capacity:	89 long tons at 80 ft. radius 75 long tons at 104 ft., 6 in. radius
Crew:	Up to 15

115 Ton

Builders:	Bollinger Shipyards, Lockport, La.
Length overall:	220 ft.
Beam:	80 ft.
Draft:	7 ft. (loaded)
Displacement:	Not yet determined
Crew:	2 warrant officers, 13 enlisted for 24-hour operations.

U.S. Army/Steve Harding

The 115-ton BD is operated from a small control cabin *(at top left)* located atop a tower fixed to the roof of the main winch housing. In addition to the main hoist, the 115-ton BD also has a 25-ton auxiliary hoist and a 5-ton whip hoist.

FB-814

Over the years, many thousands of cadets at the U.S. Military Academy at West Point, N.Y., have been introduced to Army watercraft during short voyages undertaken aboard the largest vessel in the school's small fleet.

The craft, the only one of its type in Army service, is the twin-screw passenger ferry FB-814. And though the portly vessel cannot hope to match the dazzling speeds of the Army's two other dedicated ferries — the Kwajalein-based catamarans Jera and Jelang K — she offers a history and dignified charm all her own.

Built in 1958 by Marinette Marine Corp. of Marinette, Wis., FB-814 was based on a double-deck excursion-boat design common at that time. Officially dubbed Design 6013, she was built to carry Army personnel and government employees between Brooklyn Army Terminal and the Caven Point Army Depot on the New Jersey shore (near Ellis Island and the Statue of Liberty). Her layout is strictly utilitarian: there are passenger seats both inside her lower, enclosed main deck house and on the open boat deck just aft of her small pilothouse. When all her seats are full, she can embark some 150 passengers.

FB-814 maintained her Brooklyn-New Jersey service until transferred to the control of First Army in 1959. She then embarked on a new mission, carrying passengers between New Rochelle, Conn., and the Army's Fort Slocum, on David's Island in western Long Island Sound. When that installation closed in 1967, the still-capable ferry was transferred to the control of West Point's Harborcraft Division at South Dock.

FB-814 now spends her days carrying USMA cadets, school employees and family members up and down the historic Hudson River, ranging as far as Constitution Island. She and the other passenger vessels of the Harborcraft Division — the 40-

The only vessel of its type in Army service, FB-814 was built in 1958. Based on a then-common double-deck excursion boat design, the ferry was initially used to carry Army employees between Brooklyn Army Terminal and the Caven Point Army Depot in New Jersey. FB-814 arrived at West Point in 1967.

passenger Q-7860[1] and the 34-passenger J-3761 (*which see)* — also support official school functions and the cadets' introduction to matters maritime. Once the official missions are satisfied, members of the USMA community may charter the gracefully aging FB-814 for recreational outings on the Hudson.

With the wholesale retirement of the 1950s-built tugs and other craft that were her contemporaries in Army service, FB-814 holds the distinction of being one of the oldest watercraft still active in the Army fleet[2]. And, given the care and attention lavished on her by the members of West Point's Harborcraft Division, she looks set to soldier on for years to come.

The ferry's primary mission is carrying West Point cadets, school employees and family members up and down the Hudson River. She also supports official school functions, and is occasionally chartered to civilian organizations for social functions.

Specifications

Builder:	Marinette Marine Corp., Marinette, Wis.
Length overall:	65 ft., 6 in.
Beam:	23 ft.
Draft:	5 ft. (loaded)
Propulsion:	Two General Motors 6-71 diesels, each generating 165hp
Speed:	11 knots (loaded)
Crew:	3
Passengers:	150

[1] West Point's Q-boat is a nonstandard vessel. Built in 1981 as a lobster boat, it was seized by the U.S. Coast Guard in 1983 while being used to smuggle drugs. It was then turned over to the academy as a replacement for an older J-boat that had reached the end of its useful life.

[2] While FB-814 was the only vessel of her design to serve in the Army, Marinette built several examples for civilian operators. At least two remain in service with Casco Bay Lines of Portland, Maine.

Kwajalein Ferries

Among the more exotic members of the Army's fleet are the high-speed, catamaran passenger ferries operated at the Ronald Reagan Ballistic Missile Defense Test Site at Kwajalein Atoll in the Marshall Islands. These vessels — *Jera* (FB-816), *Jelang K* (FB-817), *Pvt. Sorenson* (FB-222) and *Pvt. Anderson* (FB-223) — are of two types, and are the only such vessels in Army service.

The earlier of the two ferry types, *Jera* and *Jelang K*, were manufactured in Washington state by Nichols Brothers under license from the Australian firm International Catamaran Designs Pty. Ltd. *[now known as InCat and the builder of the Army's HSV and TSV prototypes, which see]* and have been in service at Kwajalein since the 1990s. Their sharply-raked superstructures house both lower passenger sections and upper pilothouses, with additional passenger seating and open deck areas. Though they differ slightly in overall dimensions, both vessels are essentially identical in design and layout, and each can accommodate a maximum of 232 passengers.

Representative of a class of high-speed, shallow-draft ferry that has found increasing favor with commercial operators worldwide, *Jera* and *Jelang K* maintain a daily shuttle service among those islands of the Kwajalein group that house range facilities, primarily Roi-Namur, Meck, Ebeye and Kwajalein itself. The catamarans are normally limited to voyages within the lagoon, though at some 1,100 square miles, that amounts to a considerable operational area.

Given the advancing age of *Jera* and *Jelang K*, the Army is in the process of replacing the vessels with the *Pvt. Sorenson* and *Pvt. Anderson*. The new catamarans are similar in layout and size to the older ferries, and were built in Australia by NQEA to a Crowther design. The *Pvt. Sorenson* was transported to Kwajalein aboard the RTS-based *Great Bridge* (LCU-2021) in November 2004, while the *Pvt. Anderson* was scheduled to arrive at the atoll as this book went to press.

Though Army-owned and designated, the ferries (like all the vessles based at Kwajalein) are operated by civilian contract crews.

Specifications

(Jera, Jelang K)

Builders:	Nichols Brothers Boat Builders, Whidbey Island, Wash.
Length overall:	76 ft. (Jera) 72 ft. (Jelang K)
Beam:	29.3 ft. (Jera) 28.5 ft. (Jelang K)
Draft:	5.5 ft.
Gross weight:	60 tons
Propulsion:	Two Detroit Diesel/GM 16V 92TA diesels, each generating 990 hp
Speed:	22 knots (loaded) 28 knots (light)
Range:	200 nm
Crew:	4 to 5

(Pvt. Sorenson, Pvt. Anderson)

Builders:	NQEA Australia Pty. Ltd., Cairns, Queensland
Length overall:	74.1 ft.
Beam:	27.5 ft.
Draft:	3.6 ft.
Propulsion:	Four Detroit Series 60 diesels, each generating 600 hp, driving four Hamilton HJ362 waterjets
Speed:	28 knots (loaded) 30 knots (light)
Range:	270 nm
Passengers:	149
Crew:	6

(Left) **The older Kwajalein ferries, *Jera* and *Jelang-K*, were built in Washington state by Nichols Brothers, under license from their Australian designer, and have been in service since the 1990s.**

(Below) **Similar in general layout to the older ferries, *Pvt. Sorenson* and *Pvt. Anderson* were designed and built in Australia and then transported to Kwajalein aboard the *Great Bridge* (LCU-2021).**

Crowther Design Pty. Ltd.

Fore and aft sheer identify this barge as a Design 231. variant, which also has hull skegs for greater stability in ope water. This particular barge is carrying folded sections of floating causeway, and is being tended by a side-loadabl warping tug.

BARGES

In a very real sense, barges are the unsung heroes of the Army's fleet. Plain, unassuming and decidedly low-tech, they nonetheless perform a variety of important roles, ranging from the transport of vehicles and equipment to the carriage of water, fuel and lubricants. All Army barges can be towed or loaded aboard larger vessels as deck cargo.

There are currently some 37 barges in the Army inventory, consisting of four major types and several designs. The type classifications (and subtypes) are:

BC: Barge, Deck Cargo, Non-propelled

There are two subtypes of the basic BC. The first, Design 231A (Barge, Deck Cargo, Non-propelled, Ocean Towing) can be towed in the open sea because it has fore and aft sheer and hull skegs that give it added stability.

This design was built in lengths varying from 120 to 142 feet and beams from 33 to 58 feet. Most surviving examples were built in the 1950s by Wiley Manufacturing Co. in Port Deposit, Md. and have been overhauled and modified as needed. On example of the larger, 142-foot variant is designate BOC and is part of the small Army watercraft flee based at Kwajalein Atoll in the Marshall Islands.

The second BC type is the Design 7005 (Barge Deck Cargo, Non-propelled, Harbors and Inland Water-

Two Design 7005 barges form the basis of a floating comman post during a riverine warfare exercise in North Carolina. Equippe with tents and power generators, the barges can be moved by SLWTs or LCM-8s.

ways) which is, as its unwieldy Army designation indicates, intended for use in sheltered waters. This barge is particularly suited for transporting vehicles, since it has a flush deck with no shear fore or aft. It also has no skegs, making it easy to maneuver in ports whose piers are in close proximity to one another.

BCDK: Conversion Kit, Barge, Deck Enclosure

This designation applies to those Design 231A barges that have been fitted with a removable deckhouse used to protect sensitive cargo from the elements. The deckhouse structure consists of 35 sections that form a watertight transverse bulkhead forward and two watertight longitudinal side bulkheads. The top of the deckhouse is pierced by one large and four small hatches, and each side bulkhead has two sliding doors. There is one watertight door in the forward bulkhead and a double sliding door in the aft bulkhead. Only one barge — the Army Reserve's Tacoma, Washington-based BCDK-6204 — is presently fitted with the enclosure.

BG: Barge, Deck or Liquid Cargo, Non-propelled

A variant of the basic Design 231A barge, the Design 231B and 231C vessels each have six watertight internal tanks with a total capacity of 188,416 gallons, and are used to transport fuel, other liquids or general cargo in harbors and inland waters. The barges are each fitted with two aft skegs to improve their towing performance, and are easily recognizable by their small aft deckhouses.

An aggressive maintenance program has kept these barges — most of which were built in the 1950s and 1960s — in excellent condition. This is fortunate in that the Army Watercraft Master Plan (AWMP) envisions these craft becoming increasingly important as fuel carriers for the proposed fleet of theater support vessels. The Army inventory included 11 BGs as of mid-2004.

L/CPL T.A. Pope, USMC

A more common mission for the Design 7005 barges is carrying cargo containers, generator sets or vehicles along inland waterways or within harbors. The 7005 is easily recognizable by its lack of fore and aft sheer, which also allows easily loading of wheeled and tracked vehicles.

BK: Barge, Deck or Liquid Cargo, Non-Propelled, Knockdown (Design 218E), and Barge, Deck Cargo, Non-Propelled, Sectionalized, Nesting (Design 7001)

Though they share the same designation and are both intended for use in harbors and inland waterways, the two BK types are quite different.

A smaller and less capacious liquid carrier, the Design 218E barges each consist of two coupled longitudinal sections and can be disassembled for easier shipment by rail or ship. All four of the examples currently in the Army inventory are based at the U.S. Military Academy at West Point, N.Y.

The Design 7001 barges are intended only for dry cargo or vehicles, and consist of eight coupled transverse sections. The sections can be "nested" for rail or marine transportation. Both of the barges of this type now in use are assigned to the Army Reserve in Tacoma, Wash.

Specifications

BC (Design 231A, BOC and BCDK):

Length overall:	120 ft. 142 ft. (BOC)
Beam:	33 ft. 58 ft. (BOC)
Draft:	2 ft. 6 in. (loaded) 8 ft. (BOC)
Displacement:	760 long tons (loaded)
Deck cargo capacity:	585 long tons

A variant of the basic Design 231A barge, the 231B and 231C vessels are used to transport fuel, other liquids or general cargo in harbors and inland waters.

(Design 7005):

Length overall:	110 ft.
Beam:	32 ft.
Draft:	7 ft. 6 in. (loaded)
Displacement:	690 long tons (loaded)
Deck cargo capacity:	570 long tons

BG:

Length overall:	120 ft.
Beam:	33 ft.
Draft:	8 ft. (231B) 8 ft. 6 in. (231C)
Displacement:	763 long tons
Deck cargo capacity:	578 long tons
Liquid cargo capacity:	4,160 barrels

BK:

Length overall:	45 ft. 9 in. (Design 218E) 81 ft. (Design 7001)
Beam:	18 ft. (218E) 17 ft. (7001)
Draft:	1 ft. 8 in. (loaded) 1 ft. 6 in. (7001)
Displacement:	33 long tons (loaded) (218E) 181.3 long tons (loaded) (7001)
Deck cargo capacity:	20 long tons (218E) 180 long tons (7001)
Liquid cargo capacity:	225 barrels (218E)

L/CPL T.A. Pope, USMC

An LCM-8 tends a Design 7005 barge that is loaded with Marine Corps generators and cargo containers. The landing craft has the barge on a hip tow, which is feasible in broad inland waterways. The barge can also be husbanded by the ST-900 and LT-100 tugs.

And sometimes the barge can return the favor. Here an LCM-8 is loaded aboard a Design 7005 barge for transportation from Fort Eustis to a nearby civilian dockyard. In this configuration the barge would most probably be towed astern of a tug, rather than being hip-towed by another LCM.

West Point cadets use the academy's J-3761 to practice riverine operations on the Hudson River. One of only two Design 4003 J boats in the Army inventory, this vessel is also used for passenger transportation and special events. The J-boat assigned to the 17th Area Support Group in Japan, J-3793, is identical in layout.

MISCELLANEOUS CRAFT

Small Craft

In addition to its larger and better-known landing ships and high-speed vessels, the Army also operates several types of small service craft. These range from patrol boats at high-security installations to workboats and small harbor craft, and they range in age from nearly ancient to fairly recent.

J Boats

In the Army vessel-designation system both utility boats and picket boats carry the letter J before their hull numbers. At the time of writing, the Army's inventory included 11 J-designated vessels of three separate types.

The two older vessels are designated Boat, Picket, Design 4003. Built in fairly large numbers from the 1950s to the late 1970s, the Design 4003 boats are steel hulled and of classic "cabin cruiser" layout — a small foredeck, recessed cabin with extensive glazing, and an open and recessed aft deck.

The older J boats literally serve worlds apart. J-3761 (built in 1954) is based at the U.S. Military Academy at West Point, N.Y., while J-3793 is assigned to the 17th Area Support Group in Kure, Japan. The former has spent its entire service life at West Point and is used primarily for passenger service and special events, while the latter undertakes a range of administrative and harbor-master duties.

The newer J boats are of two types. The first is a 26 foot, 200hp, single-screw vessel that looks something like a sport fishing boat. It has a small cabin, the after end of which forms the pilot-house enclosure, and the deck is fitted with extensive handrailing. Eight of these boats are used for security-patrol and general-utility work at Aberdeen Proving Ground, Md. The sole example of the second type of newer J boat is of similar outline, but is longer (43 feet) and is fitted with a 460hp engine. This boat is assigned to dive-support and range-patrol duties at the Army's Kwajalein Atoll missile range complex in the Marshall Islands.

One of many types of small boats used for miscellaneous duty, the bridge-erection boat is actually intended for use by engineer bridge companies. Small yet powerful, these boats have even seen service as armed patrol craft on the rivers of war-torn Iraq.

U.S. Army/Steve Harding

Q-Boats

The sole remaining example of this type, Q-7860, continues to soldier on as a part of the U.S. Military Academy's Haborcraft Department at West Point, NY. Like the ferry FB-814 and the J-3761, Q-7860 is used primarily for passenger transportation on the Hudson River.

Workboats

The Army also uses various types of smaller craft as tenders aboard larger vessels and for miscellaneous duties in harbors. These include a variety of designs, ranging from the standard "workboat, lifesaving and firefighting" to inflatable Zodiac types (found aboard LCUs and LSVs, for example) to small aluminum "bass boat" craft. Also common are bridge-erection boats, whose normal job is erecting and tending the floating bridges constructed by Army combat-engineer units.

Given the vast amount of ocean that the Kwajalein range encompasses, it's not surprising that USAKA

(Below) The largest of U.S. Army Kwajalein Atoll's small service craft is SR-001. Though designated as a search-and-rescue vessel, it is also used for security patrols, personnel transport and diver support. One of USAKA's smaller boats is tied up to starboard of SR-001.

U.S. Army/Steve Harding

(U.S. Army Kwajalein Atoll) has three boats of two types not found elsewhere in the Army. While both types are locally designated as search-and-rescue vessels, they are also used for general patrol work, personnel transport and diver support. The larger of the three (designated SR-001) is 51 feeet long and powered by twin 600hp Detroit diesels, while the other two boats (*Guardian 1* and *Guardian 2*) are 24 feet in length and powered by twin 115hp outboards.

Specifications

Design 4002 J Boats:

Length:	46 ft. 4.5 in.
Beam:	12 ft. 3 in.
Propulsion:	Twin 165bhp diesels
Crew:	4-6

Aberdeen PG J Boats:

Length:	26 ft. 6 in.
Beam:	8 ft. 6 in.
Propulsion:	One 200hp diesel
Crew:	2-4

USAKA J Boat:

Length:	43 ft.
Beam:	15.5 ft.
Draft:	3.5 ft. (loaded)
Propulsion:	One 460 hp General Motors 8V-71 diesel
Crew:	4-6

Workboat, Lifesaving and Firefighting:

Length:	26 ft.
Width:	7 ft. 4 in.
Draft:	1.3 ft.
Propulsion:	One 55hp turbocharged diesel
Crew:	2-3

USAKA SR-001:

Length:	51 ft. 9 in.
Beam:	14 ft. 2 in.
Draft:	3 ft.
Propulsion:	Twin 600hp Detroit 8V-92 diesels
Crew:	2-4
Passengers:	Up to 24

USAKA Guardians:

Length:	24 ft. 7 in.
Beam:	7 ft.
Draft:	16 in.
Propulsion:	Twin 115hp Evinrude outboards
Crew:	2-4

Bridge Erection Boats (Mk II):

Length:	27 ft.
Beam:	8 ft. 2 in.
Draft:	1 ft. 8 in
Propulsion:	Twin diesels driving waterjets
Crew:	2-4

NONSTANDARD VESSELS

WORTHY

Perhaps the most specialized vessel in the Army's fleet is the former Navy ocean-surveillance ship *Worthy*. Originally built to aid in the Cold War effort to identify and track Soviet submarines, the stout vessel has instead made a name for herself as a long-serving member of the Marine department of the Ronald Reagan Ballistic Missile Defense Test Site (universally referred to as RTS) on Kwajalein Atoll in the Marshall Islands.

One of 18 *Stalwart*-class vessels built in the late-1980s, *Worthy* and her sisters were based on the design of the T-ATF fleet tugs operated by the Navy's Military Sealift Command. The vessels were equipped with the Surveillance Towed Array Sensor System (SURTASS) and were used to collect, process and transmit underwater acoustical data that allowed Navy shore facilities to detect and track both diesel- and nuclear-powered submarines. *Worthy* was placed in MSC service in December 1988, but by the early 1990s the Navy's changing strategic needs in terms of submarine tracking led to the decommissioning of the entire *Stalwart* class.

The ships didn't stay idle for long, however. Ruggedly built, with abundant electrical-generation capability and offering generous berthing and working spaces, the vessels soon found a host of new occupations. Some went to foreign governments, several were transferred to other U.S. federal agencies for use in the nation's ongoing maritime drug-interdiction efforts, and still others became specialized research vessels.

That, at first, seemed to be *Worthy's* fate. Struck from the Naval Register in May 1993, she was transferred to the U.S. Geological Survey for use as an oceanographic/geological research vessel, to be homeported in Redwood City, Calif. Naval architects at the firm of M. Rosenblatt and Son developed detailed alteration drawings and specifications for her conversion, but unforeseen funding problems that developed after the USGS's acceptance of the unconverted vessel from the reserve fleet put her conversion on hold.

U.S. Navy

One of 18 *Stalwart*-class ocean-surveillance vessels originally intended to help track Soviet submarines by collecting, processing and transmitting underwater acoustical data gathered by the SURTASS system, *Worthy* was commissioned into the Military Sealift Command in 1988. The *Stalwart*-class design was based on that of the Navy's T-ATF fleet tugs.

U.S. Army/Steve Harding

Fortunately, it was at this point that a new and unexpected player entered the game. Raytheon Range Systems Engineering Co., a division of the Raytheon defense-systems firm, needed a suitable vessel upon which to embark a mobile range-safety system for use at the RTS.

Lying some 2,500 miles southwest of Hawaii, the test site encompasses the 100 small islands of Kwajalein Atoll and more than 1,100 square miles of ocean. Ballistic missiles fired from the continental United States, and smaller devices launched from Hawaii and other Pacific islands, impact within the atoll's vast lagoon (the world's largest). To ensure that commercial aircraft and vessels do not interfere with missile tests, and vice versa, Raytheon developed the Kwajalein Mobile Range Safety System (KMRSS).

Embarking the KMRSS aboard *Worthy* required some modifications to the vessel. The most obvious change was the addition to the ship's aft superstructure of two large white domes housing redundant telemetry antennas, each of which supports S-band receiving gear and a UHF Flight Termination System transmitting antenna. Other modifications included additional cabling, upgrades to *Worthy's* heating and air-conditioning systems, and improvement of the ship's original engine cooling-water system. In order to meet the more stringent government regulations governing research vessels, *Worthy* was fitted with an additional watertight bulkhead, 30 long tons of ballast were placed within her double hull and the capacity of her ballast tanks was equalized.

Worthy[1] entered service with the RTS Marine Department in 1996, joining a small Army-owned, contractor-operated fleet that includes single examples of both LCU-2000 and LCU-1600-class vessels,

Worthy's mission on Kwajalein required extensive modifications, the most obvious of which was the addition of two large domes housing telemetry antennas. The vessel also was fitted with additional accommodation spaces, given upgraded heating and air-conditioning systems, and painted in high-visibility white.

two catamaran passenger ferries, several LCM-8s and various small boats *[see the separate entries for those vessel types for additional details]*. In addition to her ongoing KMRSS mission, *Worthy* occasional undertakes other radar-tracking assignments and continues to provide billeting support for operations at remote launch sites.

Specifications

Builders:	Trinity/Halter Marine, Gulfport, Miss.
Length overall:	224 ft.
Beam:	43 ft.
Draft:	14.5 ft.
Displacement:	2,300 tons
Propulsion:	4 Caterpillar D398 diesels, each generating 970hp
Speed:	11 knots (max)
Range:	4,000 nm
Crew:	12 to 16

[1] Like the other Army vessels on Kwajalein, *Worthy* operates on a Table of Distribution and Allowances (TDA) status and "belongs" to the U.S. Army Space and Missile Defense Command. Unlike the tugs *Gulf Condor* and *Mystic*, however, *Worthy* was never given an Army hull number and her name is preceded by "KMRSS" rather than "USAV."

CURRENT FLEET LIST

High-Speed Craft

Hull Number	Name
TSV-1X	*Spearhead*
HSV-X1	*Joint Venture* (when under Army control)

Logistics Support Vessels

Hull Number	Name
LSV-1	*GEN Frank S. Besson Jr.*
LSV-2	*CW3 Harold C. Clinger*
LSV-3	*GEN Brehon B. Somervell*
LSV-4	*LTG William B. Bunker*
LSV-5	*MG Charles P. Gross*
LSV-6	*SP4 James A. Loux*
LSV-7	*SSG Robert T. Kuroda*
LSV-8	*MG Robert Smalls*

Large Tugs

Hull Number	Name
LT-101	*Gulf Condor*
LT-102	*Mystic*
LT-801	*MG Nathanael Greene*
LT-802	*MG Henry Knox*
LT-803	*MG Anthony Wayne*
LT-804	*BG Zebulon Pike*
LT-805	*MG Winfield Scott*
LT-806	*COL Seth Warner*
LT-1974	*Champagne-Marne*
LT-2076	*New Guinea*
LT-2085	*Anzio*
LT-2096	*Valley Forge*

Small Tugs

Hull Number	Name
ST-901	*Dorchester Heights*
ST-902	*Pelham Point*
ST-903	*Fort Stanwix*
ST-904	*Green Springs*
ST-905	*Scholarie*
ST-906	*Sag Harbor*
ST-907	*Appomattox*
ST-908	*Sackets Harbor*
ST-909	*Bunker Hill*
ST-910	*Santiago*
ST-911	*Enduring Freedom*
ST-912	*Fort Moultrie*
ST-913	*Restore Hope*
ST-914	*Mulberry*
ST-915	*Cat Lai*
ST-916	*Desert Storm*

Landing Craft, Utility
(LCU-1600 Class)

Hull Number	Name
LCU-1667	*Manassas*
LCU-1673	*Double Eagle*

Landing Craft, Utility
(LCU-2000 Class)

Hull Number	Name
LCU-2001	*Runnymede*
LCU-2002	*Kennesaw Mountain*
LCU-2003	*Macon*
LCU-2004	*Aldie*
LCU-2005	*Brandy Station*
LCU-2006	*Bristoe Station*
LCU-2007	*Broad Run*
LCU-2008	*Buena Vista*
LCU-2009	*Calaboza*
LCU-2010	*Cedar Run*
LCU-2011	*Chickahominy*
LCU-2012	*Chickasaw Bayou*
LCU-2013	*Churubusco*
LCU-2014	*Coamo*
LCU-2015	*Contreras*
LCU-2016	*Corinth*
LCU-2017	*El Caney*
LCU-2018	*Five Forks*
LCU-2019	*Fort Donelson*
LCU-2020	*Fort McHenry*
LCU-2021	*Great Bridge*
LCU-2022	*Harpers Ferry*
LCU-2023	*Hobkirk*
LCU-2024	*Hormigueros*
LCU-2025	*Malvern Hill*
LCU-2026	*Matamoros*
LCU-2027	*Mechanicsville*
LCU-2028	*Missionary Ridge*
LCU-2029	*Molino Del Ray*
LCU-2030	*Monterrey*
LCU-2031	*New Orleans*
LCU-2032	*Palo Alto*
LCU-2033	*Paulus Hook*
LCU-2034	*Perryville*
LCU-2035	*Port Hudson*

Floating Machine Shop

Hull Number	Name
FMS-789	*Vulcan*

Barge Derrick
(BD-100 Class)

Hull Number	Name
BD-6074	*Naples*
BD-6701	*Big Bethel*

Barge Derrick
(BD-115 Class)

BD-6801	*Keystone State*
BD-6802	*Saltillo*
BD-6803	*Springfield*
BD-6804	*Delaware*

Passenger Ferries

FB-814	
FB-816	*Jera*
FB-817	*Jelang K*
FB-222	*Pvt. Sorenson*
FB-223	*Pvt. Anderson*

Range Safety Vessel

(no hull number)	*Worthy*

Landing Craft, Mechanized,
Mod. 1 (These Vessels Not Named)

LCM-8500	LCM-8560
LCM-8502	LCM-8580
LCM-8505	LCM-8581
LCM-8515	LCM-8582
LCM-8520	LCM-8583
LCM-8521	LCM-8584
LCM-8522	LCM-8585
LCM-8523	LCM-8586
LCM-8524	LCM-8587
LCM-8525	LCM-8588
LCM-8526	LCM-8590
LCM-8529	LCM-8591
LCM-8535	LCM-8592
LCM-8536	LCM-8593
LCM-8538	LCM-8597
LCM-8540	LCM-8598
LCM-8541	LCM-8599
LCM-8542	LCM-8601
LCM-8543	LCM-8602
LCM-8544	LCM-8603
LCM-8545	LCM-8604
LCM-8546	LCM-8605
LCM-8548	LCM-8607
LCM-8549	LCM-8608
LCM-8550	LCM-8609
LCM-8551	LCM-8610
LCM-8552	LCM-8611
LCM-8553	LCM-8612
LCM-8555	LCM-8613
LCM-8556	LCM-8614
LCM-8557	LCM-8615
LCM-8558	LCM-8616
LCM-8559	LCM-8618

Landing Craft, Mechanized,
Mod. 2 (These Vessels Not Named)

LCM-8594	LCM-8595
LCM-8596	LCM-8600
LCM-8696	LCM-8617

Utility/Picket Boats
(These Vessels Not Named)

J-3761	J-7855
J-3793	J-7856
J-7850	J-7857
J-7852	J-7858
J-7853	J-7862
J-7854	

Work Boats

Q-7860	(not named)
SR-001	(not named)
(no hull number)	*Guardian 1*
(no hull number)	*Guardian 2*

Barges
(These Vessels Not Named)

Deck Cargo, Non-propelled:

BC-184	BC-6260	BC-6467
BC-528	BC-6262	BC-6548
BC-529	BC-6266	BC-6550
BC-6159	BC-6283	BC-6612
BC-6164	BC-6316	BC-6619
BC-6168	BC-6461	
BC-6188	BC-6465	

Conversion Kit, Barge, Deck Enclosure:
BCDK-6204

Deck or Liquid Cargo, Non-propelled:

BG-1906	BG-6442	BG-6453
BG-6084	BG-6446	BG-8505
BG-6087	BG-6447	BG-8506
BG-6227	BG-6448	

Deck or Liquid Cargo, Non-propelled, Knockdown

BK-8327	BK-8469	BK-8477
BK-8336	BK-8472	BK-8479

Side-Loadable Warping Tugs
(These Vessels Not Named)

SLWT-26	SLWT-85-013
SLWT-27	SLWT-85-014
SLWT-28	SLWT-85-015
SLWT-29	SLWT-85-024

Bibliography

Published Books

Friedman, Norman: "U.S. Amphibious Ships and Craft, An Illustrated Design History." Naval Institute Press, Annapolis, Md., 2002.

Gibson, Charles Dana: "Marine Transportation in War, The U.S. Army Experience, 1775-1860." Ensign Press, Camden, Maine, 1992.

Grover, David H.: "U.S. Army Ships and Watercraft of World War II," Naval Institute Press, Annapolis, 1987.

Harding, Stephen: "Great Liners at War." Motorbooks International, Osceola, Wisconsin, 1997.

Magazine, Journal and Newspaper Articles

n.a.: "Ships of the Army," in Military Review, July 1946, pp. 11-20.

Black, William M., and Dale A. Hueber: "Army Watercraft Operations in Southwest Asia," in Transportation Corps magazine, September 1991, pp. 10-14.

Dao, James: "Odd Vessel Serving Allies as Truck Stop That Floats," in the New York Times, April 3, 2003.

Harding, Steve: "Training Army Mariners," in Soldiers magazine, April 2001, pp. 18-22.

______________; "Sail Army…Fast," in Soldiers, February 2003, pp. 30-35.

Knox, T.M.: "The Work of the Army's Fleet," in Quartermaster Review, March-April 1930, pp. 23-29.

Nichols, Roger L.: "Army Contributions to River Transportation," in Military Affairs, April 1969, pp. 242-248.

Patterson, Kristin: "History in the Making: The Army Takes to Sea," in Army Times, March 3, 1997, pg. 19.

Steele, Dennis: "The Army's Quick Cats," in Army Magazine, November 2002, pp. 54-55.

Manuscripts, Official Documents, Special Studies and Unpublished Sources

King, David L.: "United States Army Watercraft Listing." Prepared for the Office of the Chief of Transportation by International Consultants, Inc., St. Louis, Mo., 1996.

Larsen, Harold: "The Army's Cargo Fleet in World War II," U.S. Government Printing Office, Washington, D.C., 1945.

Masterson, James R.: "U.S. Army Transportation in the Southwest Pacific Area: 1941-1947," U.S. GPO, Washington, D.C., 1949.

Rauch, Dale A.: "Amphibious Ships and Landing Craft," U.S. Army War College, Carlisle Barracks, Pa., 1987.

U.S. Army, Combat Developments Command: "Analysis of Lighterage for Discharge of Vessels," 1966.

__________, Combined Arms Support Command: "HSV-X1 (Joint Venture) U.S. Army Snapshot, 20 MAR 2002-13 July 2002," Fort Lee, Va., January 2003.

__________, Military Traffic Management Command: "Joint Venture (HSV-X1) Load Planning and Transportability Analysis," Newport News, Va., September 2002.

__________, Office of the Chief of Army Reserve: "The Army Watercraft Restructuring Plan, Army Reserve Implementation Plan," July 2002.

__________, Office of the Chief of Transportation: "Transportation Corps Vessel Characteristics," Fort Eustis, Va., 1953

___________: "The Transportation Corps 1959 Watercraft Fleet," Washington, D.C., October 1959.

____________: "Registry of Army Vessel Names," Fort Eustis, 1987.

____________: "Army Watercraft Master Plan." Fort Eustis, 1997.

____________: "Army Watercraft Master Plan." Fort Eustis, 2002.

____________: "Registry of Army Vessel Names," Fort Eustis, August 2003.

U.S. Army Transportation School: "Harbor Craft and Inland Waterways," Fort Eustis, September 1966.

U.S. Army Tank-Automotive Command: "Army Watercraft Restructuring Plan Divestiture Update," Warren, Mich., May 2002.

___________: "Advanced Concept Technology Demonstration: Theater Support Vessel Management Plan," May 2003.

U.S. Army, 469th Transportation Detachment: "USAV Spearhead (TSV-1X), Load Planning Guide and Standard Operating Procedures," May 2003.

U.S. Army: Army Regulation (AR) 55-530, "Hospital Ships," December 1943.

_________: AR 56-9, "Watercraft," 2002.

_________: Field Manual (FM) 55-15, "Transportation Reference Data."

__________: FM 55-105, "Water Transportation: Oceangoing Vessels," September 1944.

__________: FM 55-130, "Small Boats and Harbor Craft," January 1944.

_________: Technical Manual (TM) 55-510, "Amphibious Lighter Operator's Handbook."

________: TM 55-511, "Operation of Floating Cranes."

_________: TM 55-1905-202-12, "Operation of LCM-8 Mod. 0 Landing Craft."

_________: TM 55-1905-217-12, "Operation of LCM-8 Mod. 1 Landing Craft."

_________: TM 55-1905-220-14-1, "Landing Craft, Utility, LCU-1600 Operator's Manual."

_________: TM 55-1915-200-10, "Logistics Support Vessel Operator's Manual."

_________: TM 55-1925-204-12, "100-Foot Tug Operator's Manual."

_________: TM 55-1930-203-10, "Lighter, Amphibious (LARC-LX) Operator's Manual."

_________: TM 55-1940-201-12, "Boat, Picket, Operator's Manual."

U.S. General Accounting Office: "Better Planning and Management of Army Watercraft Could Improve Mission Capability While Reducing Excess Numbers and Cost," Washington, D.C., August 1979.

Other books by Stephen Harding

Gray Ghost: The RMS Queen Mary at War
Dominator: The Story of the Consolidated B-32 Bomber
(with James I. Long)
Air War Grenada
U.S. Army Aircraft Since 1947
Great Liners at War (Vol. I)

These books are available through your favorite bookseller, or from the publisher.

Forthcoming books:

Great Liners at War (Vol. II)
Fly Army

Visit our Web site, **www. sail-army.com**, for updates on these titles.